VGM'S Complete Guide to

Career Etiquette

From Job Search Through Career Advancement

Mark Satterfield

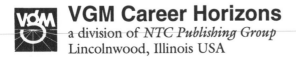

VGM Career Horizons
a division of *NTC Publishing Group*
Lincolnwood, Illinois USA

Library of Congress Cataloging-in-Publication Data

Satterfield, Mark
    VGM's complete guide to career etiquette : from job search through
career advancement / Mark Satterfield.
       p.   cm.
    ISBN 0-8442-4471-6
    1. Business etiquette.   I. Title.
HF5389.S28   1996
650.1—dc20   95-30143
                                          CIP

To Mom and Dad, who taught me the fundamentals of etiquette.

Published by VGM Career Horizons
A division of NTC/Contemporary Publishing Group, Inc.
4255 West Touhy Avenue, Lincolnwood (Chicago), Illinois 60646-1975 U.S.A.
Copyright © 1996 by NTC/Contemporary Publishing Group, Inc.
Printed in the United States of America
International Standard Book Number: 0-8442-4471-6

19   18   17   16   15   14   13   12   11   10   9   8   7   6   5   4   3   2

CONTENTS

INTRODUCTION: CAREER ETIQUETTE FOR THE NINETIES

Careers are complex entities. Challenging one minute, deadly dull the next, it is impossible to predict what the next step will be on the career ladder. The potential stumbling blocks are numerous, and negotiating passage is a Herculean task. Given the complexity of careers, it is not surprising when individuals decide that the grass must be greener at some other company. Thus, the résumé is dusted off, the headhunters contacted, and the job search underway. If successful, this activity results in a new work assignment that is exhilarating for the honeymoon period. However, all too often, the issues of discontent that were evident in the previous job crop up again in the new position. What is the career-minded worker to do?

Before you consider making a job change, do everything possible to maximize the potential of your current position. The following suggestions may help you reinvestigate a stalled career. They are also worth keeping in mind as you begin *any* job—even if it's your first.

- **Work on important projects.** Important projects help increase the market share or profitability of your company. For example, if you are in the personnel department, important projects might include recruiting salespeople to sell insurance or training them to sell more products. Conversely, activities such as administering safety reports or handling employee complaints do not directly contribute to the bottom-line success of your company.

  If you are involved in important projects you will derive a greater sense of satisfaction from and be more enthusiastic about your work. Influential managers will also tend to notice your efforts and think of you as a valuable contributor.

- **Work for the right people.** Being the protégé of a fast-track or highly respected senior manager can boost your career farther and faster than any other single source. Hard work, determination, and effort count for little if your activities are overshadowed by a boss who is viewed as going nowhere but down.

   How do you determine who the right people are? Be astute to the political winds. Pay attention to who is running the important areas of the company and tap into the corporate grapevine to hear who the management winners and losers are. Try to get to know people who are viewed favorably by the organization on both an informal and a formal basis and suggest ways you might be able to contribute to the company.

- **Demonstrate initiative.** Senior managers often criticize their employees for not demonstrating initiative. View your assignments as a challenge, offering you an opportunity to add creative input to projects. If the final result reflects your personal contribution, you will feel more pride in the results and be happier about your job.

   Okay, you've been told before that initiative is important. But what exactly does management want when it asks for more initiative? After all, if I show initiative and decide to change suppliers on my own, the result may be that I no longer *have* a job, let alone this job I'm not terribly enamored with. Management defines initiative this way:

   1. Identifying opportunities before anyone else does.

   2. Accepting challenges and responsibilities eagerly.

   3. Plunging into assignments independently and with enthusiasm.

   4. Being excited by the prospects of beginning a project, exhibiting high energy, and showing a willingness to be involved.

- **Remember good ideas can surface any time.** Successful managers will tell you that they never really stop thinking about the business they're in. They know that good ideas can pop up driving to work, at the dinner table, or working in the yard. They never tell themselves, "I don't want to think about business."

   Take a lesson from these managers and keep yourself open to ideas on how you can improve the effectiveness of your area of responsibility. Think about how what you read or observe can be applied to your work. Remember that good ideas are fleeting. Have you ever awakened in the middle of the night with a great idea you know you won't forget? Come dawn, most of us can't remember what it was that seemed so unforgettable at the time. Solution: Keep pads of paper and pens next to your favorite chairs and your bed or in the car.

If you think creatively about new ways to approach your work, two things will happen. You will start to enjoy your job a lot more, and your productivity will increase. Remember, senior management loves people who increase productivity.

Having said all that, it's still easy to get frustrated. Take the case of my friend Martha. She was justifiably frustrated. After graduating from college in May with a degree in business, lots of extracurricular activities, and a good grade point average, she is still without a job. Despite numerous on-campus interviews, networking with everyone she knows, and sending out enough résumés to kill a large forest, she is no farther along in her job search than she was at graduation.

Tough times often require unique actions. Simply doing what everyone else is doing won't help you break away from the pack. Employment agencies are inundated with résumés, help-wanted ads draw unprecedented numbers of responses, and candidates are often tripping over themselves in their networking efforts. Remember, there are no absolute rules when it comes to job seeking—so don't be afraid to do something different. The result is far more important than the process.

Certainly, not everyone will feel comfortable pursuing alternative methods such as putting their résumé on a signboard and parading it around the streets of a major city, and these tactics would be well beyond the boundaries of appropriate career etiquette. However, there are some less radical ideas that can help you improve your odds.

Remember, job search etiquette does not require that all your contact with a company be through its human resources department. In fact, you may be better off bypassing this department whenever possible. The premise being that personnel staff can't hire you—all they can do is either refer you to the hiring manager or nix your chances for further interviews. Thus, you're better off dealing with the hiring manager from the beginning. However, this strategy carries with it the risk of alienating the human resources staff. Although these people don't carry much weight in many organizations, it doesn't normally require much weight to torpedo your candidacy.

The first step is to find out who the hiring supervisor is. Since it's unlikely that human resources will give you the person's name, you'll have to use alternative approaches. Business directories, such as *Standard & Poor's* and *Dunn & Bradstreet*, can often point you to the right people. Also, check publications produced by your local trade or professional organization. Associations usually publish a membership list that includes names of employers and job titles.

Another tactic is to focus on lesser-known organizations. Everybody and their brother applies to the highly visible Fortune 500 companies. It's very difficult to make your background stand out if your résumé is one of hundreds washing in with the tide. You've got a much better chance of receiving individual attention if you apply to the smaller companies in your area. This is where employment growth is taking place.

One of the difficulties of applying to smaller companies is finding them; most don't emblazon their names on countless billboards and ads. However, with a little bit of investigation you should be able to target companies that offer good opportunities and aren't as competitive as the larger, more well-known employers. *Inc.* magazine publishes a list of the fastest-growing employers each October; it's available in most public libraries. The Chamber of Commerce publishes the *Major Employers Listing*, which provides information on both large and small companies. Both are effective resources to target companies that aren't on every job seekers hit list. Pay attention to articles published about your industry. Don't hesitate to call up the writer if you read a particularly interesting story. Most authors are flattered by such calls and can be a valuable resource on job leads. Writers can usually be contacted through their publications. Finally, check with the research librarian at your local public library. He or she can help you identify some of the smaller faster-growing companies in your area.

You should also consider taking a temporary assignment. The ranks of temporary workers have grown tremendously in recent years. The criteria for obtaining a temporary assignment is usually less stringent than for full-time work, so you may find it easier to break in. The major attraction of temporary work is that it often leads to a full-time assignment. Check the Yellow Pages under "Temporary Employment Agencies" to find firms specializing in your field. Many larger companies have created in-house temporary departments. Getting registered usually requires little more than filling out an application.

One final tip for finding work in this competitive economy is to not immediately reject a job just because you think it's beneath you. It's important to take a long-term approach to your career. Working as an administrative assistant or secretary may not be a bad move if there is an opportunity to progress. In some of the more popular and competitive fields many of today's senior managers started out as clerks.

What Are Employers Really Looking For?

One of the most perplexing problems facing job changers is trying to figure out what companies are really looking for in candidates. The problem is an acute one, especially for seasoned managers. Since the typical interview lasts only 30 minutes, that's precious little time in which to talk about those aspects of your background that are of most interest to the interviewer.

Of course, every company has its own unique criteria to evaluate candidates. Ultimately, the personal chemistry between you and the interviewer is the most important component. Candidates sometimes make the mistake of trying to adapt their personality to the perceived personality of the interviewer. Career counselors are unanimous that this is a major error. In most cases you won't be able to pull it off, and as a result you will come across as indecisive, confused, or worse. Even if you're successful in convincing the interviewer that you are "his or her kind of person," it will likely backfire in the end. Adopting a different personality in a 30-minute interview is one thing. Sustaining the charade over an extended period of time is virtually impossible. Remember, if you're eliminated because of a bad "fit," it probably was, in fact, a bad fit.

The downsizing of corporate America has placed an increased emphasis on a candidate's interpersonal skills. Today's manager must deal with an increasingly disenfranchised group of employees. He or she is apt to be supervising workers who wonder if they are the next to be laid off or who haven't received much of a pay increase in recent memory. You'll score points by discussing specific examples of situations where you built morale, productivity, and team work.

Working for a variety of companies, as long as it's not carried to an extreme, is also viewed positively by many companies. Of particular appeal are candidates who have experience working in both large and small companies. As downsizings continue, the remaining management jobs are increasingly complex. Individuals who have the broad-based perspective gained from working in a variety of business situations will be increasingly in demand.

Another by-product of the "leaner" corporations of the '90s is a lack of staff support. This is true even for senior-level executives. For example, it's not unusual today for top managers to share secretaries. Managers must also be able to make business decisions without convening multiple task forces to study a problem. However, in order for today's managers to function in this new environment, they must be able to quickly access information on their own. This means they must be computer literate.

Companies are looking for people who are willing to be held accountable for their individual contributions. This is reflected in the modern compensation plan. At many companies, the base salary is relatively modest and the majority of a manager's income comes from bonuses or through opportunities to purchase stock in the company. International experience also is increasingly valued by many companies.

And what about the total quality management (TQM) movement? Has this popular management initiative translated into specific hiring criteria?

The feedback is mixed. Some companies believe that experience in TQM methodology is beneficial. Others think that the underlying principle behind the movement—improving customer service—is the most important criteria. Total quality management has reinforced the importance of managers delegating responsibility to others. Whether you call it TQM or simply improved customer service, this is a hot button in many organizations. If you've played a role in making your company more responsive to the needs of its customers, make sure you mention it in an interview.

Computer familiarity, increased emphasis on interpersonal skills, a focus on customer service, and a willingness to take responsibility for your actions are all on the top of the list for what businesses need most in their managers. Articulating specific examples of when you have demonstrated these traits can give you a competitive advantage in your next interview.

A New Perspective on Career and Job Search Etiquette

It's clear that in order to succeed in the '90s, you have to develop a portfolio of skills that can be marketed readily to a variety of companies in different industries. To compete in today's competitive arena, you have to develop a new mind-set on how the career game is played. For example, one of the traditional symbols of career success has been an organizational title; a goal for many individuals was to have the words "vice president" appear on their business cards, and success was measured by its attainment. In the work environment of the '90s you can forget about working for a title. There are countless unemployed vice presidents who spent too much time trying to become vice president rather than developing a solid base of marketable business skills.

These days employers are less concerned with what you are called than with what you can actually do. Thus, it is imperative that you develop a repertoire of skills that can be marketed both internally to your company and externally to the business community at large. An unfortunate reality is that you never know when you may be required to conduct a job search. The business skills you bring to the party will largely determine your employability. Examples of useful skills might include a knowledge of IRS rules, how to set up a warehousing system, how to work effectively with the Japanese or how to develop computer systems. The more business skills you possess the greater your career options.

Another critical component for career survival is developing contacts both within and outside your company. Although everyone has heard the term *networking* and knows that it is the method by which most jobs are found, most people wait until their job is in jeopardy before they make a concerted effort to develop business contacts. Think about developing contacts in three areas: 1. Identify individuals who might have a positive impact on your career and cultivate relationships with them. 2. Identify trade groups or business associations that will enable you to broaden your base of contacts by developing relationships with people doing similar work in other industries. 3. Join a local business organization, such as your local chamber of commerce or business association. These organizations enable you to meet businesspeople with whom you would otherwise never come in contact.

The role of continuing education in career success cannot be underestimated. This does not necessarily mean going full-time to graduate school, although that may be a wise decision for some individuals. At a minimum, take courses that will keep you current on developments in your field. This is especially important for experienced managers who are primarily in a supervisory role. Chances are you will be more marketable if you retain your technical competence along with developing strong supervisory skills. You never want to become outdated in your field. Additionally, by participating in a continuing education program, you'll have the opportunity to broaden your contact base.

The type of job you perform for your company is critical. Individuals whose jobs impact the bottom line are much more valuable than those in staff assignments. If you are in a support role, think about how you can contribute in the most meaningful way possible. You should lobby for an opportunity to work in one of the critical areas of your organization. Those who have spent their entire careers in support roles will be the first to be let go if business falls off.

Be cautious about group assignments. Whereas this type of work is increasingly popular in business, it makes it more difficult for the individual to shine. In a group situation, you must be perceived as a good team player and still have your individual contributions recognized. One trick to becoming the team player with the greatest amount of visibility is to volunteer to write up meeting minutes, prepare a final report, or summarize the group's recommendations. The person who writes the report is invariably the one who garners the greatest amount of recognition.

If you are in middle management or a high-level position, establishing a relationship with a management recruiter or headhuner can be a valuable piece of career insurance. You can develop a good relationship with executive recruiters by introducing them to individuals who might become either candidates or clients.

An old option, moonlighting, has become increasingly attractive for the career-mobile individual. Although moonlighting is normally frowned on by many employers, it is an effective method by which to test out an alternative career. Budding entrepreneurs often find that moonlighting represents an opportunity to test out an idea without the risk of depending on the entrepreneurial venture as their sole means of support. Obviously, you should avoid businesses that represent a direct conflict of interest with your current employer.

As we've discussed, in the '90s your career success will be determined by the skills you possess, your contacts, and your ability to maintain a variety of career options. Now, more than ever, you will find that you are ultimately responsible for the success of your own career. The perceived security of working for a large corporation is largely an illusion. Today, savvy employees try to develop a career survival kit of marketable skills and contacts so that if the handwriting appears on the wall they will read the message accurately and be prepared to reenter the job market.

Part One

❧

JOB SEARCH
ETIQUETTE

CHAPTER 1

SURVIVING THE FIRST STEPS OF A JOB SEARCH

The number of companies announcing layoffs or reorganizations continues to grow. While many closings receive a lot of publicity, many businesses have quietly laid off pockets of employees. When you receive the news that your job has been eliminated, the reality of unemployment hits home. Regardless of whether you saw the layoff coming, the actual termination notice is a sobering experience. Feelings of helplessness and confusion are very common. Although you may feel overwhelmed at this point, there are some etiquette guidelines that can help you make sure your job search gets off to the best possible start.

Communicate

You're not in this alone. Your spouse and children are likely to be as concerned about the future as you are. It is important that you hold a family meeting and talk about what has taken place. Fear of the unknown can be reduced by open and frank discussions about why the layoffs took place and the steps you will be initiating to secure a new position. While the tone of these conversations should be positive, you should also be realistic in communicating that the job search may take some time.

Prepare Emotionally

Most of us progress through our day-to-day activities on an even keel. We tend not to experience extreme highs or lows of emotion. However, losing your job can upset that equilibrium. Don't be surprised at experiencing wide emotional swings ranging from anger to depression to optimism. Realize that your spouse is also likely to experience similar emotional swings although they may occur at different times.

Review Your Finances

Now is the time to take a practical look at your severance package, other sources of income, and anticipated expenses. Cut back reasonably but not excessively. For example, maintaining health or business club memberships is a good idea. You'll want to have a place to work off stress and stay in shape. Additionally, business and social clubs can be excellent networking sources. Vacations generally should be deferred. Take a vacation as a reward once you have accepted a new position.

One of the first concerns facing the newly unemployed is financial. How will the mortgage be paid? How long can we survive financially? Implementing a job search campaign is feasible only after basic decisions about what to do with retirement money, severance pay, medical coverage, and unemployment benefits have been made. Many outplacement consultants say that by addressing the financial issues first, you will be able to progress and focus your energies on obtaining a new position.

A good place to start assessing your financial situation is your former employer's benefits department. The staff are normally very helpful and can provide good advice on what your various options are. Be wary of the financial advisors who start advertising in the newspaper once a layoff is announced. If you wish to use the services of a financial planner, get referrals from people you respect who have worked with the advisor over an extended period of time.

Severance packages vary depending on your level in the company and length of employment. A typical package is one week of pay for each year of service, with a maximum amount set by company policy. It is common for senior-level managers to receive three to six months pay. It is normally advisable to take the severance pay in one lump sum. This gives you greater control of how you spend it. However, if you are laid off near the end of the year, you might wish to extend the payout into the following year, because severance is taxable in the year it is received. You will most likely want to put the money in something liquid such as a money market account, so you have access to the cash for short-term expenses.

Financial advisors often recommend that you not cash out your 401(k), profit-sharing, or other tax-deferred retirement plans. The argument against this is that you pay taxes on the earnings plus a 10-percent federal tax penalty if you are under the age of 59½. This could amount to a tax penalty of forty percent. A number of the larger 401(k) plans offer you the option of keeping your money in your former employer's plan. In fact, many employees have no choice but to have their pension money remain in their former company's plan until retirement. If you do take your retirement money with you when you leave, financial professionals advise putting it into an individual retirement account with a mutual fund, bank, or brokerage house.

Health insurance coverage is an area that needs to be addressed quickly. Although health insurance may be cut off at the time of termination, federal law requires employers to offer medical insurance to departing employees at group rates plus 2 percent for up to 18 months. This coverage is not inexpensive. Another option is, if your spouse works, moving to his or her plan if you are eligible.

Laid off individuals often fail to apply for unemployment payments. You should realize that unemployment compensation is an entitlement and not beneath you. The payments are based on a percentage of your gross income.

Being laid off can be an initially devastating experience. Developing a financial plan is an important first step. Once money issues are resolved you will be able to focus on the important task of finding a new position.

Set Goals

Most of us acknowledge that goal setting is important. However, it's a little like losing weight; we know we should do it, but it's easy to procrastinate. However, if you don't discipline yourself to set realistic and attainable career goals, you're likely to achieve only a fraction of your potential.

Goal setting is often difficult because we don't know where to start. A helpful tool in setting goals is to think of the word "smart," and associate each letter with a requirement for your goals. By using the following method you'll be able to set both career and personal goals that are challenging and achievable.

- S stands for *specific*. Goals must be specific. If you can't articulate your goals or write them down, they're not detailed enough. If a goal is only a fuzzy notion in your head, it's likely to remain little more than a dream. An example of a specific career goal might be "to implement a customer service survey within the next six months" or "be ranked among the top 10 percent of sales reps in my company." These are specific goals that allow you to focus continually on what you are trying to accomplish. Goals such as "I want to be the best customer service rep ever" are too vague because the meaning of "best" varies from person to person.

- M stands for *measurable*. Goals have to be measurable, otherwise you won't know if you've achieved them. The key to establishing measures is to break your overall goal into components and set measures for each subgoal. For example, your overall goal might be to increase your visibility with your company's senior management. A subgoal would be to participate in two task forces on subjects important to senior management in the first quarter of the year.

- A stands for *agreed upon*. This refers to the fact that career goals can't be established in isolation. It's important that you get input and support from others, including your family, co-workers, and boss. Most supervisors react extremely positively to a request to discuss career goals. It's important that you do your homework before the meeting. You'll find the discussion more productive if you take the time to think about your strengths and developmental needs. The more you are prepared to brainstorm about specific career possibilities, the more beneficial the meeting will be. As part of your preparation, make sure you consult your spouse or significant other. Make sure that your career goals are compatible with your personal and family goals.

- R stands for *realistic*. A career goal to become president of your company may not be realistic, depending on your background, training, and motivation. On the other hand, a goal of getting to work on time every day wouldn't appear too terribly challenging. You'll need to use your good judgment and business savvy to determine how realistic your goals are. Set the bar high enough so the goal is challenging and stretches your capabilities, yet not so high that you're simply setting yourself up for failure.

- T stands for *time framed*. Again, you'll want to break down your overall career goals into subgoals and assign a time frame for each component. A typical career goal might have a six-month or one-year time frame; for example, "By this time next year my goal is to be fully proficient in the following five data processing programs. . . ." Once an overall goal is set, you'll need to establish interim deadlines for the various components such as, "Develop proficiency in software program #1 within the next three months." Assigning time frames to the components will help you stay on track and focus on the goal.

Don't keep your goals to yourself. The more you tell others about your goals, the greater your likelihood of actually achieving them. Writing down your goals and communicating them to other people are proven powerful techniques to eliminating procrastination.

Review Your Career Options

Too often, individuals facing unemployment immediately focus on getting interviews. This is usually a mistake. Take some time and reflect on what you really want to do in your next position. Although experiencing a layoff is unpleasant, it is an opportunity to examine a variety of career options. Think about which aspects of your job gave you the greatest amount of satisfaction and what were your major sources of frustration. Strive to maximize the former and minimize the latter.

If your company does not offer you outplacement assistance, ask for it. With the economy as it is, laid off employees need all of the help they can get. An outplacement firm can help you sort out your career options and will provide valuable assistance on how you can best market yourself to prospective employers.

Sometimes participating in a battery of vocation-oriented tests can help. Finding out what you want to do in life is never easy. For many of us, it's an issue we continually revisit. What was important to us when we were 20 is different from what we need when we're 40. Unfortunately many of us "fall" into jobs or careers because a friend chose a similar path, our parents urged us in a particular direction, or it seemed like a good idea at the time. One accountant commented that he initially chose accounting in college because it was in the front of the course catalogue. He mused that if he had started in the back of the catalogue he might be a zoologist today.

Testing

Deciding on the job that best fits your personality and ambitions is a process of self-discovery. The first step, narrowing down your options, is the most difficult. We often attempt to make career choices through the process of elimination. Many MBA students, returning to school after a couple of years' work experience, fall into this category. They may say, "I really don't know what I want to do, but the one thing I do know is that I don't want to do what I was doing before I came back to graduate school." Unfortunately this process-of-elimination method tends to be time-consuming and not very practical. If you're wrestling with what type of work is best suited to your tastes, testing may be of help.

Tests or, as they're called in the trade, assessment instruments come in a wide range of choices. Remember, no one test or combination of tests will pinpoint exactly the type of work at which you'll be best, but they can be helpful in sorting out possibilities. One important point is to make sure you have a professional interpret the test results for you. Otherwise, the data can be a little confusing.

One of the most common (and oldest) instruments is the Strong Interest Inventory. The Strong compares your answers to a series of questions with those of literally thousands of individuals in a variety of occupations. While the results can give you some interesting insights, you'll want to have a professional walk you through the feedback. For example, the results of my Strong showed that my responses were very similar to those of funeral directors and bakers. This was somewhat disconcerting until my counselor drew out the themes (small businesses, entrepreneurial nature) behind my results. The data then made a lot of sense.

Another popular instrument is the Myers-Briggs Type Indicator. It is often administered in conjunction with the Strong. It assesses your personality type based on eight factors, such as introversion and extroversion. The Myers-Briggs can help you define the type of culture in which you'll fit most comfortably.

After the Myers-Briggs and the Strong, assessment instruments become a little freeform. There are dozens and dozens from which to choose. Each instrument tends to focus on a particular issue although there is a certain amount of overlap. That's not necessarily bad, since it provides you with validation and consistency. Some of the instruments commonly used include:

- **(COPES)** *Career Occupational Placement Evaluation Survey*. This instrument assesses your values and motivations and addresses your problem-solving skills.

- **(CAPS)** *Career Ability Placement Survey*. This instrument provides an assessment of your occupational skills and may pinpoint areas to develop.

- **(CRIS)** Among other things, this tool measures issues that may cause you stress on the job.

- **California Psychological Inventory** *(CPI)*. This test assesses your leadership and management capabilities.

If you're interested in taking vocational tests, there are a number of options. The placement office at your alma mater sometimes offers this service. There are also a number of programs available to the public at local colleges. Plan to spend $130 to $150, which will include a battery of tests and a follow-up session to interpret the results.

Develop Your Résumé

You inevitably will face the task of putting together your résumé. Keep some important basics in mind. First, it's impossible to create a résumé that everyone will think is perfect. You'll drive yourself absolutely crazy if you try to incorporate every individual suggestion and idea. While a résumé is important, many job seekers spend far too much time tweaking and changing what is essentially an acceptable document. No one is going to rule you out because you used ten-point rather than eight-point type, or one page rather than two. A résumé is an advertisement. It can't get you a job; its purpose is to get you interviews. Focus your résumé on your accomplishments rather than your job responsibilities. Ultimately, employers are less concerned with what your were responsible for than they are in what you achieved.

Practice Interviewing Skills

Sad to say, most people think they interview better than they actually do. Spending some time with a career consultant who will videotape you in a mock interview is a good investment. You may be surprised at how you come across. At a minimum, obtain a list of the most commonly asked interview questions and practice answering them out loud. You'll find there is a world of difference between thinking to yourself how you would answer a question and actually articulating it.

A unique instrument has recently come to the market specifically to help you develop your interviewing skills. The Interview Insight Report gives you a sense of how you come across in an interview. It also give you suggestions for questions to ask and specific questions to be prepared for based on your personality type. At only $35, it's a great tool for anyone in the midst of a job change. The Interview Insight Report can be ordered from Corporate Insights & Development at 404 728–4741.

Develop a Contact List

What you read about networking is true. The largest percentage of jobs are filled through this source. Networking is simply the process of making sure people are aware you are actively looking for a new position. A good networking tip is not to contact your most promising prospects first. You'll become more comfortable with the networking process once you've had a couple of trial runs. Practice your pitch on your second-string contacts.

Avoid Procrastination

Procrastination can be a real obstacle to a job search, because it's so easy to think up excuses to do nothing. It's so much easier just to complain about the current situation then it is to actually do something. Identifying the worst case scenario (perennial unemployment) doesn't take a great deal of imagination and can cause even the most motivated of us to sink into the abyss of inaction.

Procrastination is an especially difficult issue for job seekers who are three months, six months, or even longer into their searches. What started out as a quest for new opportunities can quickly settle into a routine of nonreturned phone calls and an endless stream of "In the unlikely event that hell does freeze over, we would be glad to reconsider your application" letters. Given the negative feedback that unfortunately is part and parcel of the job search experience, overcoming the dreaded inertia of procrastination becomes critical for success.

This is all well and good. But, how exactly do you maintain motivation and persevere when the only feedback you've received in the last couple of months has been negative? While there aren't any simplistic solutions that work for everyone, some general good advice from the experts may help keep your spirits up when they're particularly lagging. Wayne Dyer, in his popular book *Your Erroneous Zone*, offers some sensible tips to overcome procrastination.

1. **Live 15 minutes at a time**. By this, Dyer refers to the fact that 15 minutes of work on your job search (or any difficult project) is better than no effort at all. This is along the same lines as 15 minutes of exercise is better than no exercise at all, or a small tax refund is better than no refund at all. What may happen is that after committing to work on a project for "only" 15 minutes, you become motivated to work on it longer.

2. **Designate a specific time for a task you've been putting off**. Although most of us keep a daily calendar and a to-do list, we usually don't do a good job of coordinating the two items. Our to-do lists almost always become lists of those things we'd accomplish if only we had some extra time. Not surprisingly, we get frustrated when we don't get everything on the to-do list done. If you're serious about getting your to-do list done, you've got to plan when you're

actually going to do the work. As Dyer correctly points out, if you don't mark on your calendar when you're going to work on tasks, they won't get done.

3. **Work in small steps**. One of the reasons we put off important projects is that we don't where to begin. For example, an early step in the job search process that's easy to procrastinate about is putting together your résumé. Actually sitting down and trying to write a résumé from scratch can be a fairly daunting task. To avoid procrastination, you need to break the task down into small steps that can be implemented easily. These might include:

   • Go to the bookstore or library and get books on résumé writing for format ideas and content suggestions.

   • List all jobs held since college in chronological order.

   • List three accomplishments for each job held in the past ten years.

   By breaking large projects down into smaller steps, you'll find it's easier to actually get started on your important projects.

4. **Tell others or write it down**. There is an enormous psychological benefit in communicating to others what you've been procrastinating about. Opera star Luciano Pavarotti credits losing 100 pounds to the fact that he went on a television talk show and said he was going to do it. Many people have found that their resolve increases if they tell others about their personal goals. Although writing down your goals is a powerful tool for heightening motivation, telling others is even more effective. An additional benefit is that the people you tell will tend to ask you how you're proceeding toward that goal. This subtle form of self-induced peer pressure is a wonderful motivator.

Sharpen Time Management Skills

If you're like a lot of job seekers, you find that your priorities can shift dramatically between Friday afternoon and Monday morning. In fact, you may find that your priorities change between Monday morning and Monday afternoon. The nature of a job search requires flexibility. However, if you don't efficiently manage your time, you'll quickly discover that your search is managing you, rather than vice versa. The key to success is getting organized.

The first step in managing your time is to focus your energies on the right projects. Just because you're doing a lot of work doesn't mean you're actually accomplishing a whole lot. A good first step is to write down the four key priorities you want to accomplish tomorrow. These might include "Fax my résumé to Mr. Harvey at Acme Distributing for the sales job," or "Call Ms. North first thing in the morning concerning the lead I picked up from Tim." Time management experts recommend that you conduct this exercise at the end of the day rather than first thing in the morning. Having just completed today's work helps you focus more clearly on what you need to accomplish tomorrow.

Determining what's important is another key factor in managing your time well. You can spend all morning licking stamps on envelopes for your mass mailing, but that's probably not the most productive use of your time. Actually making that networking call to your friend Joan's referral is more important, but it's easy to put off. It's human nature to want to defer the difficult tasks and spend your time on projects that are more passive and less threatening.

A tip to help you determine the order in which to do projects is to think about what's urgent and important. If it's urgent and important (such as faxing a résumé to a prospective employer from a hot lead you just got) put it on the top of your list. If the project's not urgent or important (putting stamps on envelopes for a mailing), postpone it until you complete your more important projects.

To increase your effectiveness and efficiency in your job search, block out certain times of the day for different activities. If morning are when you write best, allocate that time for job search correspondence. If the afternoon if when you really start to feel motivated, this is when you should schedule your networking calls. We all have different biological rhythms and times of day when performing certain work is easier. Try to schedule your activities for the time you're most productive.

Managing the telephone is another important key to increasing your effectiveness and using your time wisely. Try to make your calls within blocks of time. Place five to six calls at once rather than only one or two. Sometimes it's difficult to get motivated to make those prospecting calls you know you have to do. Experts say the first call is actually the most difficult. After that, you'll tend to get into a "telephone swing" and the process becomes a lot easier. Take advantage of the momentum and place multiple calls at once.

If you try to call between the hours of 10:00 A.M. and noon or 2:00 and 4:00 P.M., you'll probably only hear, "I'm sorry, Mr. Smith is in a meeting." You can decrease the odds of playing a prolonged game of telephone tag by making your calls either first thing in the morning, from 11:30 A.M. to noon, or after 4:00 P.M. Although this increases the likelihood of actually contacting the party you're trying to reach, a certain amount of telephone tag is inevitable.

Another tip in managing the phone is to ask, "When would the best time be to reach Ms. French?" You'll normally find that secretaries are quite helpful about informing you of the best time to call back. An additional benefit of this tactic is that it allows you to maintain control of the process. When you initiate the call, you can have all your notes in front of you and be well prepared.

Job search etiquette includes careful attention to all of the components listed in this chapter and numerous others. The more you feel that you are doing the "right thing," the greater your chances for success. Managing your time is critical to maintaining control over your job search. The more in control you feel, the less stress you'll feel and the more productive you'll be.

CHAPTER 2

DEALING WITH OUTPLACEMENT FIRMS

You may meet them sooner than you think. With each week bringing news of more layoffs, outplacement consultants find themselves extremely busy. Given these uncertain economic times, it's a good idea to understand exactly what outplacement consultants do.

A Brief History

It is interesting that until about 15 years ago there was no outplacement industry. Outplacement, as in industry, grew rapidly during the 1980s, as companies reduced their middle management ranks. Today, the number of outplacement firms has grown significantly. They include both national firms and local organizations.

There were two precursors to today's outplacement profession. The first was the emergence of industrial and organizational psychologists in the 1950s and 1960s. These individuals offered highly specialized services to corporations, including psychological evaluations of applicants and counseling of employees whose performance was not meeting company standards. The 1960s also saw the emergence of firms that marketed their job change services to individuals. Unlike executive search firms, which worked for paying client companies, these executive marketing firms advertised that they would help the job seeker obtain a new position. They relied heavily on newspaper ads that were carefully written to avoid the outright promise of a new job. The thrust of their service was that for a significant fee a candidate would learn to become a more proficient job seeker.

These executive marketing organizations sold a concept that was very attractive to potential job seekers, yet was shrouded in controversy. Due to the large sums they charged individuals and the questionable nature of what they actually delivered, these firms found themselves in frequent trouble with the Better Business Bureau and other consumer watchdog organizations.

Although the concept of charging managers for assistance in looking for new job had been around for years, the breakthrough that created the outplacement industry was getting corporations to pick up the tab. By selling the benefits of such services to employers, the outplacement industry was born. The benefits to the company were primarily twofold. Companies do not want discharged employees hanging around the office, potentially spreading the seeds of discontent. Providing outplacement services enables a company to quickly remove an employee from the premises. Having a displaced manager conduct his or her job search from the outplacement firm's office lets the rest of the staff focus on current business rather than the plight of the affected individual. The second benefit was that by contracting for outplacement services, companies purchased visible evidence that they cared about the welfare of their employees. This message was particularly reassuring to the remaining members of the workforce.

If you're offered outplacement assistance, consider it a blessing. Don't make the initial assumption that your job search will be a breeze and that the help of experts isn't available. You're likely to regret that assumption down the road.

Choosing a Firm

If outplacement assistance is part of your severance package, you may have the opportunity to select from a short list of "approved" firms. This is difficult for many people. What differentiates one outplacement firm from another can be subtle. First impressions are sometimes erroneous. Remember, the assistance you'll need immediately after getting the bad news is going to be different from the resources you'll require when your search is stalled after six months. If you're given a choice of firms, don't take that choice lightly.

An outplacement firm can provide a wide variety of services. What you will be offered depends on what your company is willing to pay. You may wish to investigate the following types of services:

Secretarial services/word processing. Is there a limit on the number of letters you can send out? What is the turnaround time for typing? Is there any limit on postage? If overnight delivery is needed, how is it handled?

Telephones. Is there any limit on calls? How are long distance calls handled? How are incoming phone calls handled?

Reference materials. Does the company have current editions of important directories, such as *Standard & Poors* and *Dun & Bradstreet?* Does it have subscriptions to the business periodicals and relevant journals?

Résumé preparation and printing. Most firms teach you the basics of how to prepare a résumé. If you don't like the firm's style, can you substitute your own? Is only one type paper provided, or do you have a choice?

When evaluating an outplacement firm, be sure you learn about the extent of support it offers. Basic programs include a review of the job search fundamentals and preparation of your résumé. The next level includes one-on-one follow-up to ensure your search stays on course. Videotaped mock interviewing is an effective means to determine how you are coming across in interviews and is highly beneficial.

Another advantage of outplacement is the opportunity to have an office to go to each morning and to interact with colleagues who are in the same situation. The support you receive from other outplaced managers is a little-talked-about but very real benefit of the outplacement process.

Bill Tiffan, senior vice-president for the nation's largest outplacement firm, Drake Beam & Morin, offers some additional advice. He recommends developing a checklist of questions, such as, "How long has the local office of the firm been open?" to compare firms. You'll want a firm that has had an ongoing relationship with the local business community.

Don't be swayed unduly by the roster of companies that do business with the outplacement firm; more important are the types of people it services. Some of the larger firms, such as Drake Beam and Right Associates, can truly claim experience with a diversity of functions and industries. Smaller firms may offer exceptional service for individuals in specific industries. Make sure you ask about the firm's track record in dealing with people like yourself.

Selecting a Consultant

Don't be afraid to ask tough questions about the backgrounds of the staff. Some firms have been criticized for lax hiring standards. Being fired and having gone through an outplacement program shouldn't be an acceptable criteria for a counselor. Make sure you actually talk with the person who will be working with you. Ask about their experience and training. Top firms require their counselors to go through extensive training before they work with clients.

Outplacement consultants come from a variety of backgrounds. Many have worked in the executive recruiting business as either contingency or retainer recruiters. Organizational psychologists were among the first to enter the outplacement field. Despite the negative publicity that has surrounded the executive marketing profession, a few of the better practitioners have now switched to the corporate-sponsored side of the business. Given their inherent aggressiveness, they are often highly effective in motivating clients to explore every avenue that might result in a job lead.

How are individuals and counselors matched up? Ideally, you want someone who has had experience in your industry. This is an area in which outplacement firms often fall short. Although the process of finding a job (résumé preparation, networking, how to respond to ads, and so on) is largely the same regardless of background, the hiring climate in the defense industry is quite different than the high-technology environment. You'll want a counselor who keeps current with trends in your industry and who can offer practical advice on where you are the most marketable. If your counselor can't discuss these issues, his or her value to you is limited.

Ultimately, your choice of an outplacement firm will come down to the counselor with whom you'll be working. As Mr. Tiffan points out, this relationship is the most important aspect of the outplacement experience. A sad fact is that your job search, despite your initial optimism, is likely to last longer than you want. As the months go on and you begin to feel increasingly pessimistic about finding a new job, your outplacement counselor can spell the difference between despair and motivation. Select with care.

Career Assessment

Take the assessment component of outplacement with a grain of salt. The firms tend to put great emphasis on "discovering alternative career paths." The reality is, if you've been an engineer for the past ten years, your most marketable career path is another engineering position. Deep inside there may be a screenplay that hasn't been written, but always remember that your earning power is largely tied to what you did in the past. The career assessment component is usually most beneficial for people in dying industries or those for whom relocation is necessary but not possible.

Outplacement is a true benefit for individuals facing a layoff. As with many other services, the more you know about what is offered, the greater your likelihood of maximizing the benefit.

CHAPTER 3

NETWORKING

There probably isn't anyone out there who hasn't heard through one or more sources that most jobs are found through networking. While this is certainly true, the problem for many people is that they start networking too late or they don't realize it takes time to get a network up and running. They wait until the ax has fallen before beginning the process. Networking is more than an effective tool to find a new job. It's a fundamental tool that can help you in all of your day-to-day activities and can aid your career in innumerable ways. As noted philanthropist Gorden Gekko commented, "The most valuable thing to own is information." As a growing number of people are realizing, networking enables you to find out everything from who's hiring to where to go for a great deal on tires. Yet, for all the publicity, implementing a networking campaign remains a daunting task. Questions include: "What do I say?" "Who do I contact?" and, most frustrating, "How do I overcome this nagging feeling that I'm imposing on the people with whom I'm trying to network?"

First, let's define our terms. Networking is hardly a magical process that requires special training or unique skills. It is simply the process of using friends, former colleagues, and others in your field to provide you with information of specific assistance. They do this by keeping their eyes and ear open to opportunities they may hear about or by introducing you to their contacts who may be able to assist your career. Since success in the job search and all aspects of career management is driven, in part, by statistics, the more opportunities you hear about and the more people you meet, the greater your chances for success.

Networking is a long-term investment. If you expect immediate results from your contacts, you're bound to be disappointed. The person who opens a conversation by saying, "I do bookkeeping. Do you need any work done?" probably won't get very far. Networking relationships take time to develop. Keep the analogy of Chinese bamboo in mind. You plant it and nothing much happens for the first four years. However, with the proper cultivation, it can shoot up 50 feet in the fifth year.

One of the key advantages of learning about opportunities through networking, is that it often enables you to get a jump on the competition. This becomes apparent when you look at the process by which many companies fill open positions. The first step is to look internally to see if a suitable candidate can be found. If no candidate emerges, management will then often ask current employees for recommendations. It is at this point that networking pays dividends. If you are referred to the organization by someone in your network, you avoid having to compete with the hoards of applicants that are generated by help wanted ads and employment agency listings.

Getting in Touch

So, who do you contact? The key to successful networking in a job search situation is to target specific companies and meet as many people working there as possible. Many different doors can lead to employment at a single company. Your objective is to explore as many as you can.

The initial step in implementing your networking campaign is to develop a list consisting of your friends, family, and business contacts who you feel comfortable approaching. Most people prefer to initiate the networking process by writing a letter to each contact and then following up on the telephone. A better approach may be to send a three-page packet to each person on your list. This packet includes a cover letter, your résumé, and a separate list of the companies in which you are most interested. You might consider using the following text for your letter introduction:

> As you may have heard, our company has recently undergone a major restructuring. Although I survived the past layoffs, this one caught up with me. Thus, I am now faced with the challenge of investigating new employment opportunities.
>
> At this point, I am developing a list of contacts. It occurred to me that within your circle of business and personal acquaintances you may know of one or more persons who may be interested in receiving my résumé—a copy of which is enclosed for your perusal. Also enclosed is a list of companies I've researched that could possibly use someone with my background and experience.
>
> I would be grateful if you could share the names of anyone you know in my target companies. Of course, you never know where your next job will turn up, so if you have other contacts that may know of opportunities, I'd welcome their names also.
>
> I'll call you next Tuesday morning to discuss any suggestions you have. Thank you for your help.

Once your contact gives you a name, discuss the best method by which you can be introduced. Ideally, your contact will call or write to the person to introduce you, but this is not always feasible. At a very minimum, make sure you have your contact's permission to use his or her name when calling the referral.

An effective telephone call to a networking prospect includes the following steps:

1. State who referred you.

2. Articulate what type of job you are looking for.

3. Briefly outline why you are qualified.

Networking success depends on you being organized, concise, and direct about the purpose of your call.

Are you imposing on people? Probably not. Most people enjoy talking about their profession and are often flattered that you are coming to them for advice. Moreover, since you are being referred by someone they know and presumably respect, they will usually grant you a meeting or some telephone time.

Keeping Your Favor Bank Full

Atlanta businessman Edward St. Marks identifies people to whom he can refer business and makes sure he delivers on his promises. The implicit message is that he expects other people to return the favor at some point in time. "Most people have a great sense for the concept of the 'favor bank' and understand that if you want to make withdrawals, you've also got to make deposits. Unfortunately, there are some people who only want to take and never give. These folks tend to quickly develop a reputation and find their number of networking contacts dramatically shriveling over time."

Outplacement consultants and executive recruiters, who tend to be experts on effective networking, offer the following advice on how you can get more out of your networking efforts:

1. Remember names. This is hard for most of us. One tip is not to rush introductions when you meet a new person. Try to repeat his or her name and associate it with something to make it memorable. If you're introducing someone to a group, repeat the person's name several times during the opening minutes of the conversation.

2. Succinctly describe what you do. People tend to remember sound bytes rather than long explanations. Summarize your job in a way that is brief, yet as descriptive as possible. If the person with whom you're speaking doesn't remember what you do, it's unlikely they'll be able to refer any clients to you. Thus, rather than just saying "I'm an accountant," try, "I mostly help small businesses with their accounting problems."

3. Wait until the end of a conversation to give your business card. Some networkers evaluate the success of any meeting by the number of cards they hand out and collect. Your emphasis should be on your conversations, not on how many cards you've collected.

4. Don't overlook the competition. Some businesspeople make the mistake of intentionally avoiding meeting their competition. In reality, your competition may be a valuable resource for referral business that is too small or too far away for them. Additionally, if it does become necessary for you to conduct a job search, guess which companies may offer the best opportunity.

5. A little creativity and sensitivity can go a long way. A friend of mine, who on learning that a networking contact's daughter was recuperating at home following surgery, sent the daughter a copy of a popular Disney video and a get-well card. A class act which no doubt will pay long-term benefits.

You won't be able to help everyone all the time, but you should do some homework before going to a meeting with potential contacts. Think about the issues with which the participants are likely to be concerned and refresh your memory on potential contacts to whom you may be able to refer. Carrying a pocket-size address book with you can often help you provide an immediate referral. Remember the old saying, "Givers gain;" the people who provide the most leads and assistance also receive the most.

Internal Networking

Don't overlook the benefits of internal networking. Internal networking can both enhance your promotional opportunities and reduce the likelihood of you becoming an early casualty of a layoff or downsizing.

Networking is about developing relationships. However, developing relationships without a plan rarely yields the desired results. The goal of internal networking is to garner as much visibility for yourself as possible, while still being viewed as a team player. This requires the ability to maintain a delicate balance between being too passive or too outwardly aggressive. Too much of the former, and you'll get lost in the crowd; too much of the latter, and you'll be viewed as a prima donna.

The first step is to identify the individuals who can help your career. There are a number of criteria you can use to determine who these people are. Look for managers who are viewed positively, have a track record of developing subordinates, and work on important projects. Among all your business-related relationships, the one between yourself and your boss is the most important. Career advisors state that the amount of direct contact you have with your boss is a critical component in developing the right relationship. Boss/subordinate relationships tend to deteriorate due to too little rather than too much contact.

Bosses like to know what is going on in the areas that report to them, and they hate surprises. If your boss doesn't meet with you regularly, you should take the initiative to set up periodic meetings. Simply schedule time on your boss's calendar with his or her secretary. These meetings will have the benefit of keeping you both visible and informed. You'll find that a lot of information, gossip, and general news is passed along as a part of these conversations. You may find yourself becoming privy to otherwise confidential information. This knowledge can be of great benefit as you plan your own career moves.

In addition to your boss, you will want to establish an ongoing relationship with managers in other functional areas. This is particularly important if you work in a staff function, such as personnel. The better known you are to managers who are involved in the key areas of the business, the more secure your position is likely to be. If your company is driven by marketing, get to know the marketing and sales staff. If technology is the most important function to the success of your company, attempt to develop relationships with the engineers. Whatever department represents the driving function within your company, take steps to become known to these managers.

As you are developing your target list of individuals with whom to develop relationships, don't overlook the finance department. In fact, all workers should make an effort to develop relationships with finance personnel for two practical and important reasons. First, keep in mind Woody Allen's admonition: "When money is changing hands—be present." More than any other function, finance manages the budget and influences which departments have to bear the brunt of cost cuts. The more the finance department knows about your area and its importance to the organizations, the more likely you are to reap the benefits of the association.

Second, the finance department has the best perspective on the financial health of the overall business and knows which divisions are meeting their business goals. A lot of career success depends on timing. It's much more difficult to be viewed favorably in a division that is losing money than in one that is doing well. As you lobby to work with managers who are viewed positively within your organization, you'll also want to try to work for business units that are performing well.

How exactly do you become known to the right people? While this sounds like good advice, actually implementing the concept requires tact and initiative. Increasingly, companies are using multi-functional teams to address business problems. Similarly, task forces comprising personnel from a variety of functions are convened on a regular basis. Pitch your involvement on a task force to your boss. Mention that it would be a good developmental experience and would increase your department's visibility within the company. You may also communicate directly with a manager in another functional area about your interest in working on a cross-functional project team. As long as these requests are communicated tactfully, they are usually viewed as demonstrations of your initiative and willingness to be involved. Moreover, there are often more task forces than there are available workers, so an additional volunteer is usually welcomed.

In today's increasingly competitive business environment, you can't rely on luck for career success. After all, as the philosopher Shay put it, "Depend on the rabbit's foot if you will, but remember it didn't work for the rabbit." Your career success is likely to be enhanced by using networking in all of its forms to assist you in developing the important relationships you'll need.

CHAPTER 4

ASSOCIATIONS AND YOUR JOB SEARCH

Anita was frustrated. After receiving the news that she was about to be laid off, she dutifully attended the outplacement workshop sponsored by her company. She took the counselor's advice that 75 percent of jobs are found through networking to heart and decided to focus on developing as many contacts as possible. But, after three months, Anita had simply run out of people to contact. Having spent most of her career with one company, Anita discovered that most of her contacts either worked for her former employer or were in the midst of their own job searches. Other contacts, such as family and friends were well intentioned buy really didn't know anyone in her field. Anita grew reluctant to contact her small network again and again for fear of wearing out her welcome.

Anita's problem is hardly unique. People who have spent the majority of their careers with one company often do not have a broad base of contacts from which to draw if they become unemployed. The selection of people they know professionally is often quite limited. However, job seekers frequently overlook the valuable role associations can play in increasing their contact bases.

Associations cater to a wide variety of groups. While social organizations can sometimes be helpful, most job seekers find professional and civic organizations to be the most beneficial. The key to networking successfully is to develop contacts with people who are likely to know about openings in your field. Meeting people for the sake of meeting people is not the objective. Although it's possible your hairdresser might hear of a really great job, cultivating a bevy of hairdressing contacts serves little purpose for people outside that particular profession. Professional associations focus on either a specific function or industry, and you'll want to join both types. *Function* refers to the type of job you perform—such as accounting, human resources, sales, or data processing—whereas *industry* refers to the type of work in which your company is involved—such as consumer goods (Coca-Cola), pulp and paper (Georgia Pacific), high technology (Microsoft), and commercial banking (Chase Manhattan).

Finding the associations that cater to your profession is easy. Go to you local public library and ask the research librarian for the *Directory of Associations*. This reference book provides you with the national headquarters for thousands of associations categorized by function and industry. If a local chapter is not listed near you, call the national headquarters and ask for the local membership chairperson. This person will be glad to send you a packet of information that describes the association's size, dues, and meeting frequency.

Membership in association can be expensive, often running $200 to $400. This is a lot of money to invest, especially if your local chapter is not very active. Thus, it's a good idea to attend a meeting before you officially join. Most associations will be happy to let you do so. At the meeting, check out the number of people attending and how well the meetings is organized. Find out if there is a formal networking process or if people are largely left to themselves to make new contacts. Do members seem interested in meeting new people, or does the association primarily comprise old friends? Remember, the primary reason for joining an association if you're job searching is the networking contacts.

In addition to professional associations, you might also consider joining civic associations. These are often associations that focus on a particular geographic area. Many such associations are well organized and provide excellent networking opportunities for individuals seeking employment in specific cities. Many communities are also fortunate to have extremely active chambers of commerce, which provide an extensive series of meetings and presentations and do a particularly good job of making newcomers feel welcome.

While simply joining an association can increase your network of contacts, the real payoff comes from becoming involved in the leadership of that association. This is often easier than you imagine. Most associations have a great need for individuals to head up specific functions, such as member retention, publicity, or finance. Not only will you get a sense of satisfaction from becoming involved, your visibility within the group will be much greater.

Running out of networking contacts is a common problem for many job seekers. By becoming involved and active in professional or civic associations, you are likely to develop a substantial new network.

CHAPTER 5

WORKING WITH RECRUITING FIRMS

Functioning as intermediaries between applicants and employers, professional recruiting firms have established themselves as an important resource for job changers. The degree of professionalism and competence among recruiting firms, however, varies a great deal. Thus, it pays to know how different types of recruiting firms work and how to find a firm that's right for you.

Although recruiting firms are a viable component of a job search strategy, you should be careful not to put too much reliance on them as your primary source for job leads. It is estimated that recruiting firms fill only 20 percent of the available jobs. Make sure you supplement recruiting firms with other sources, such as answering ads in the paper and networking.

Be very skeptical of any firm whose fee is not paid by the employer. The recruiting industry has evolved to the point where virtually all reputable firms placing professionals and managers are paid by the hiring company. You should also be aware of the career marketing firms that advertise they will introduce you to the "hidden job market." The fee you pay is often substantial, and there has been a great deal of controversy over whether the services provided are worth the cost.

Choosing a Firm

The recruiting firms you want to contact fall into two groups; retained and contingency. Both types of firms are paid by the employer; however, the method by which they are paid is quite different. This difference is important since it affects how you deal with the firm.

A *contingency firm* gets paid only if the candidate they refer is actually hired by the employer. This may cause the firm to refer great numbers of candidates hoping that one will be selected. Companies may list an opening with many contingency firms, since they are only obligated to pay a fee to the firm whose candidate they hire. There is often a scramble among such recruiters to present as many candidates that meet the employer's specifications as quickly as possible. This can sometimes make you feel that you are simply a product to be bought and sold. Many people complain that contingency recruiters are impersonal and abrupt. Although this varies dramatically among agencies, it is important to remember that the fee is being paid by the employer, so the recruiting firm works for the employer not you. Although you should expect recruiters to be polite and professional, they are not in the business of providing career advice.

Retainer firms (also called executive search firms) receive their fee whether they fill the job or not. Retained recruiters liken themselves to other professionals, such as doctors and lawyers, who are paid even if a patient does not recover or a client is found guilty. Their incentive is that if they do fill the position, it is unlikely the client will use them again. Typically, retainer firms work on positions paying in excess of $50,000, whereas contingency forms work on a wide gamut of positions starting at around $15,000.

Choosing a Recruiter

The key to successfully managing a recruiting firm relationship is to find the right firm and the right recruiter. Finding the firms that specialize in your field is relatively easy. Kennedy Publications publishes what is acknowledged to be the most comprehensive registry of recruiting firms. The annual *Directory of Executive Recruiters* has separate sections on contingency and retained recruiters, and lists the firms geographically by function and industry specialization.

Identifying the right recruiter can be a little trickier. Generally, retained recruiters are older, more experienced managers and often were executives in the industries they now service. Since they work on upper middle management and senior-level positions, the overwhelming majority are highly professional.

In the contingency ranks, there is a greater disparity in the level of professionalism. Since contingency recruiters work largely on commission, the competition to produce revenue is intense and turnover within recruiting firms is often quite high. Try to work with a recruiter who has been in the business for at least two years and specializes in your function or industry. The National Association of Personnel Consultants grants its certified personnel consultant (CPC) designation to recruiters who have worked in the field for a minimum of two years and have passed an exam. Although many good contingency recruiters do not have a CPC designation, having the certification does ensure a certain baseline of competence.

Take advantage of referrals from friends and business associates on recruiters with whom they have worked. If you endeavor to identify firms that focus on your field and work with an experienced recruiter, you will find that recruiting firms can offer valuable assistance in your job search.

CHAPTER 6

GETTING APPOINTMENTS

Appointments are the life blood of your job search process. After all, it's difficult for people to hire you if they've never met you. How exactly do you obtain these important meetings?

Certainly, there are some high-risk strategies you might consider to get that all important appointment. Unfortunately, they tend to blow up in your face. For example, you may have heard about the prospective employee who lurked outside of the employee entrance asking everyone who entered if they were the recruiting manager. Or one candidate sent a letter requesting a meeting that concluded with the statement; "If you don't grant me an interview, I will be forced to kill your dog." A hapless investment banker wannabe enlarged his résumé to the size of a poster and paraded endlessly up and down the financial district wearing a sandwich board.

Most of us would never actually do anything so silly, but getting appointments in the traditional manner can often be highly frustrating. What's the line between appropriate and obnoxious behavior? Getting a face-to-face meeting requires tact and etiquette, but most importantly, it requires persistence.

Overcoming Barriers

Your letters are unanswered; your phone calls aren't returned. At a certain point in time it's a real challenge not to just throw up your hands and say, "I give up." However, as anyone who's persevered in the sales arena knows, it's precisely at this point that the cream is separated from the milk.

One of the fears that we all tend to have when trying to get appointments is the fear of making pests of ourselves. It's a fear you have to overcome if you're going to be successful. Actually, as long as you don't do anything

29

terribly strange, the odds of making a pest of yourself are pretty slim. Persistency and tenacity ultimately win out.

Why does persistence play such an important role in the etiquette of obtaining appointments? First, through shear tenacity, you may get lucky and actually get the person on the phone, which is the biggest part of the battle. Remember, most of us simply have to say no to other people, even to people we don't know. That's why so many of your phone calls aren't returned. The person knows you're going to ask them for something, and, since they hate saying no, the easiest course of action is to simply avoid talking to you altogether.

The second reason persistency works is the pity factor. As Gordon Geko said in the film *Wall Street*: "This is the kid. Calls me 58 days in a row. Ought to be a picture of you in the dictionary under persistence." Sooner or later you can, if you are tenacious enough, simply wear down the person you're trying to contact. Interestingly, the reaction is almost never "Gee, what a jerk. I wish (s)he'd leave me alone." Rather, the reaction is one of respect (even if given grudgingly) that you would continue to persevere in the face of a total lack of positive feedback.

You'll discover that most people will be helpful once you get in touch with them. This is commonly referred to as the Good Samaritan principle. Now, the Good Samaritan sometimes has to be prodded and nudged, but the desire to help others is a powerful and compelling motivation for most people. There are also some other psychological issues working on your behalf. One is ego: If you emphasize that obtaining an appointment with me is terribly important to you, you are appealing directly to my ego. It's tough to say no to someone who appears to value my advice so much.

There's also a pragmatic benefit called the "favor bank," which is becoming increasingly important in these uncertain times. It works like this: If I do you a favor, you'll owe me a favor. Even though I don't know who you are, you may have an influential/rich/powerful friend/relative/colleague who can be helpful to me. Most savvy businesspeople realize the importance of keeping their favor banks full. Favors are the coin of the realm in today's economy; we are constantly trading favors back and forth. Since you never know when you might need a favor, it's not a bad strategy to have your favor bank full at all times.

Setting Up an Appointment

All right, you're convinced that persistence is the key to getting appointments. But, you're still concerned about appearing obnoxious if you try too hard. You don't need to worry about that as long as you keep some simple guidelines in mind. Here's a scenario that's worked well for many individuals:

Step 1: Write the individual a short letter requesting a meeting. (Think one page, not five, if you're serious about it actually being read.) The letter should explain precisely what you want to accomplish in the meeting. Make sure you pick a reason other than trying to find out if there are any jobs available. If the person thinks all you're going to do is to hit him or her up for a job, he or she will avoid you like the plague. Conclude the letter with a statement such as, "I will follow up with you next week to determine the next appropriate steps." Ending a letter with "I would welcome the chance to meet with you. Please don't hesitate to call me," is incredibly wimpy. Wimps seldom ever get appointments and virtually all of them live terrible lives of servitude and despair.

Step 2: Wait three business days, then call. (Why three? Two days in the mail, one day in the target's in-basket. Less than three days and the person probably hasn't gotten around to reading it; more than three days and it's probably been forwarded on to some nameless troll in the word processing department.) Unless you get very lucky, the person won't be in. The chances of having your call returned at this stage are somewhere between slim and none.

Step 3: Wait two more business days and call again. Mention that you are following up on correspondence sent on such and such a date. Say you are going to be tied up most of the day, and ask what would be a convenient time for you to call back. Call back at the appointed time, but your target probably won't be in and probably won't return your call.

Step 4: Wait two more business days and call again. Mention the times you will be in your office.

Step 5: Write another letter. Repeat steps 2 through 5.

Egads, you say, isn't there an easier way? Actually, no. If the person you're trying to reach is busy and doesn't know who you are, it's going to take time for you to make any sort of impression on him or her. Quite frankly, the first few phone calls will roll off his or her back like so many rain drops. He or she won't acknowledge that you exist. However, through repeated messages, interspersed with letters, you will gradually burn your name into the target's memory. As time goes on and you continue to implement your plan, your target will begin to develop respect for your persistence. It is at this point that your phone call is likely to be returned.

Getting Your Target on the Phone

To increase your chances of actually getting your prospect on the phone, the time of your calls is important. Anecdotal research suggests that there are two windows of opportunity when you have the greatest chance of actually speaking with your target. The first window opens up around 11:15 to 11:30 A.M. and stays open until noon. People have completed their morning meetings and are generally in their offices waiting to go to lunch. Generally they are not engaged in substantive work at this time, which means you won't be distracting them from their primary business. (The corollary to this is that if you have to return a phone call, but you don't actually want to talk to the person, call between noon and 1:00 P.M.) The second window of opportunity begins roughly around 4:00 P.M. and, depending on the business the person is in, can remain open until 5:00, 6:00 or even 7:00 P.M. This window varies considerably depending on what industry your target is in. For example, the construction industry begins its business day early and tends to wrap up early. In other industries, such as consumer goods and pharmaceuticals, people tend to start and leave later.

An added advantage of placing your calls at the end of the day is that the gatekeeper (read secretary or receptionist) who would normally screen your call has usually left. You may be pleasantly surprised at the number of senior-level hiring managers who answer their own phones after five.

Some individuals have had good results by alternating phone messages with a periodic fax. Although receiving a fax is now becoming increasingly common, it still carries a message of urgency and importance that may separate you from other callers.

While tact and diplomacy are important in obtaining appointments, tenacity is the key. Don't get discouraged. If getting that appointment is really important to you, your assertiveness and follow-up skills will win out.

CHAPTER 7

WRITING JOB SEARCH CORRESPONDENCE

Many job seekers face the prospect of writing job search correspondence with a fair amount of trepidation. Part of the problem is making your letter stand out. Word processors have increased the ease with which you can produce job search mailings, which, when coupled with an increased number of people looking for work, results in an overabundance of paper criss-crossing in the mail. Ensuring that your letters don't get lost in the pack becomes critically important.

A lot of job search correspondence stands out for precisely the wrong reason—it's incredibly lousy. For example, I recently received a poorly photocopied cover letter in which my name had been inserted. At least the writer came close to the correct spelling of my name. Unfortunately, the concept of partial credit doesn't exist in the world of job searching. Mistakes are usually fatal. While the letter stood out, the memorable impression it made obviously wasn't what the writer intended.

One of the best ways to ensure that you don't fall into this trap is to put yourself in the reader's shoes. What would your reaction be if this letter came across your desk? Would you be enticed to learn more about the writer, or would you say "ho hum" and trash it?

There are some general letters you'll have to write as you navigate the tricky shores of the job search:

- Letters to specific individuals

- Letters requesting informational interviews

- Thank you letters following interviews

- Letters to headhunters

The goal in writing these letters is to obtain maximum impact with minimum effort. You want to use a form letter when you can get away with it and customize when it's appropriate. Of the three letters mentioned previously, the first two always have to be written individually; the third only has to be written once.

Keep the following etiquette tips in mind for each type of letter:

- Letters to specific individuals must be customized to the reader.

- If the person is well known to you, use their first name; otherwise, the more formal salutation of Mr. or Ms. is appropriate. If you do not know the individual personally, mention in the opening paragraph how you obtained his or her name and the reason for your letter. For example:

  I read with interest your comments in the *Chicago Tribune* about the impact recent environmental regulations will have on your business. As an environmental engineer with seven years experience, I thought my background might be of interest.

or

  I will be graduating from Emory University in May with my MBA. I've concentrated in marketing and am particularly interested in obtaining a position with a consumer packaged goods firm upon graduation. I obtained your name through our alumni office and was hoping that you might have 45 minutes sometime over the next two weeks to share with me how you broke into the industry after you graduated in 1985.

- Close all letters by stating when you plan on following up. Statements such as "Please feel free to contact me if you have further questions," are both ineffective and wimpy. A more effective closing line is "I'll plan on following up with you next week to determine if a personal meeting can be arranged."

This personalized format is most commonly used for cover letters and requests for informational interviews.

The Cover Letter

The cover letter should run no longer than one page and be roughly three to four paragraphs in length. Following the initial paragraph you want to highlight a specific accomplishment that matches the needs of the prospective employer. This is your primary opportunity to sell yourself and differentiate your background from that of other candidates. A common error at this point is to be too vague. Statements such as, "My superior leadership and organizational skills would be of benefit to your company," mean little to an employer. Instead, focus on briefly reviewing a specific example in which you demonstrated those traits. The body of your letter might read like this:

> A mutual associate, Susan Smith of XYZ Co., suggested that I contact you. I am in the process of changing careers and am focusing on the field of food marketing.
>
> As the enclosed résumé outlines, I have most recently worked with the advertising firm of Smith & James. As a member of the food marketing account team, I designed a marketing study to track the effect of direct-mail advertising on consumer spending. This project was completed under budget and on schedule, and should play an important role in enabling the client to increase its market share.
>
> I am confident that I can make a contribution to the goals of your marketing department. I will call you the week of January 5 to determine if an interview can be arranged.

Request for an Informational Interview

The purpose of an informational interview letter is to arrange a meeting for you to learn more about a particular industry, job, or company. Try to be creative in identifying people who are experts in their field. You will find that many people are flattered when asked to talk about what they do for a living. The text of your request might read something like this:

> I read recently in the journal *Constitution* of your promotion to vice-president. Congratulations, I wish you much continued success. I am currently in the process of investigating some new career avenues. After a great amount of thought, I have narrowed my search to the commercial banking industry.
>
> To further prepare myself, I am trying to speak personally with professionals in the field. I would greatly appreciate it if you would be able to spare a half hour to answer a few questions I have about careers in banking.
>
> I will call you next Monday to determine a mutually convenient time when we might meet.

Thank You Letters

Thank you letters need to be individually customized. The text of these letters is to summarize an interview or conversation and highlight a particular aspect of your background that most closely meets the company's needs. Thus, the thank you letter serves two purposes. It is a sign of courtesy and an effective means to remind the reader of your background. For example:

> I enjoyed our conversation yesterday and was pleased to have the opportunity to discuss my background with you. The marketing analyst position is very interesting and would represent a good utilization of my education and previous work experience.
>
> As you may recall, I recently completed a marketing study on the tire industry. My team's conclusion that safety is the most compelling reason people buy tires mirrors the theme of your current marketing campaign. I believe the skills demonstrated in preparing the study would make me a successful marketing analyst.
>
> I look forward to continuing our discussion.

Letters to Headhunters

Letters to recruiting firms do not need to be customized. The body of the letter should succinctly outline the type of position in which you're interested, your key accomplishments relating to the type of work you desire, and your salary requirements. Since your main goal in contacting recruiting firms is to be included in their database of prospective candidates, don't worry if you don't hear personally from the recruiter. Recruiters normally only contact you if they have a specific opening that meets your qualifications.

One final tip. Before you send any letter, read it out loud. If it sounds right to your ear, it's probably fine.

CHAPTER 8

ANSWERING HELP WANTED ADS

The general consensus of opinion is that help wanted advertising is an effective way of exposing you to approximately 25 percent of the jobs that are available. That's the good news. The bad news is that when you respond to an ad, you're putting yourself in competition with literally hundreds of other candidates. What's the proper etiquette to beat the odds without becoming a pest?

Blind and Open Ads

There are two types of help wanted ads: blind and open. *Blind ads* are those in which you are asked to respond to a box number; whereas *open ads* list the name of the company. Companies run blind ads for a variety of reasons; only some of which have to do with actually hiring someone. The primary advantage of blind ads is confidentiality. If the company name doesn't appear it's unlikely that applicants will show up in person to apply for the job. This has become a problem for a number of companies who are the major employers in their geographic areas. Companies that are hiring people in order to expand into new areas of business often don't want to let the competition know their intentions. Blind ads are also useful if you're planning on replacing an employee. They allow you to identify a successor before terminating the current employee.

Sometimes you see blind ads with a statement like this: "All cover letters must include complete salary history or will be immediately removed from further consideration. No Exceptions!" While this may be a legitimate request for screening purposes, it can also be an inexpensive method of conducting a local salary survey. Blind ads are also used as a check on the morale and loyalty of a company's workforce. An ad that draws a high level of response from your own organization indicates that the troops aren't feeling particularly happy.

One of the more esoteric uses of blind ads is the role they play in allowing international workers to stay in the United States. The general rule is that foreigners must have skills and abilities not found among the general population. The test for this is to run an ad with the requirements of the position to see if anyone else is as well qualified as the foreign employee. Such ads are specific to a fault and may include the exact number of years experience required on extremely specific projects. The lists are usually quite long and are tailored to the background of the individual the company wishes to retain.

If you're unemployed there's no risk in responding to blind ads, but if you're currently working you want to make sure you're not writing to your own company. That can have an adverse impact on your career progression. Err on the side of caution. If the company sounds exactly like your own, prudence may be the best course of action. If both the company and the job sound like your own it's time to move your job search into high gear.

Open ads, listing the name of the company, draw the largest number of candidates. It's not unusual for a three-by-five ad in a Sunday paper to pull as many as 300 responses. That's a lot of competition.

Composing Your Reply

No matter which type of ad you answer, look at it and make a list on what the company is looking for. This includes more than just the experience required. For example, an ad may mention the company is young and experiencing rapid growth. What does this mean about the type of person its managers need to hire? Undoubtedly, they will need an individual who is comfortable working in an unstructured environment with initiative as a key strength. You therefore need to emphasize these specific traits and give brief examples of when you have demonstrated them in your cover letter.

While the content of what you send is critical, it's important not to forget style and format. Professionalism is the most important criteria, so forget about doing something zany. You'll only wind up as fodder in some "Strangest Cover Letter I've Ever Received" file.

Obviously, cover letters can't be mass produced and require a careful scrutiny of the ad. You must read between the lines and ask yourself what type of person they really need for this job. Far too many candidates approach the job search with a "play-it-safe" attitude. They worry more about what is appropriate than how they can differentiate themselves from the competition.

The first step to increasing your odds of getting invited in for an interview is to personalize your cover letter. Simply writing "I believe a strong match exists between your needs and my background" isn't enough. You've got to be more specific. One way of illustrating your probable fit with the job is using the two-column format in your letter. Line up the requirements of the ad next to your specific accomplishments. This draws the reader's eye immediately to how your background fits the position. Alternatively, you might use a series of bullet points in your cover letter to highlight specific accomplishments.

Where and How to Look

Take advantage of all the resources that run help wanted ads. The Sunday papers carry the greatest number of ads, but don't overlook other local business publications. The *National Business Employment Weekly*, published by Dow Jones, is a good source of opportunities for managers and executives. It can be found in many drug stores and bookshops. Also check out publications produced by your professional or trade association. Ads in these newsletters and magazines will be targeted to your specific industry. If you're conducting a job search and don't belong to a professional association, now is a good time to join. You can find the appropriate organization by going to your public library and perusing the *Directory of Associations*. The fee to join is usually nominal for a local membership.

One point to remember when looking at the help wanted ads, especially in the Sunday paper, is that you've got to force yourself to read the entire section. This can be a little tedious, not to mention hard on the eyes. No, you don't have to read every ad for a nurse if you're an engineer, but you'd be surprised at where some really good ads get placed. The reason for this is that most ads are listed by the first word in the copy. Thus a job in personnel might be listed under P, T for training, H for human resources, or even I for "Innovative company seeks top human resources pro!" Since you don't want to overlook any opportunity, there really isn't any shortcut if you're going to use help wanted ads aggressively as a component of your job search effort.

You have to be a discerning reader to separate the "come-ons" from the bona fide jobs. The come-on is enticing: "Individual needed who isn't afraid to earn $100,000. Only self-motivated individuals need apply." With visions of dollar signs in your head, you make the call and schedule the interview only to learn that the "golden opportunity" involves selling water-saving shower attachments to motel chains. Plus, you have to buy your inventory up front with no guarantee that anyone will really be interested in "reducing their water consumption."

One of the frustrations job seekers face is separating the wheat from the chaff when examining the voluminous help wanted section of the paper. While no newspaper intentionally runs ads that are true consumer rip-offs, dividing the bona fide opportunities from the come-ons can be a daunting task. Fortunately, there are some signals you can pick up on to reduce the number of blind alleys you might otherwise run down.

As a general rule the more difficulty a company has in attracting candidates, the more elusive the language in which the ad is phrased. An example might be companies seeking representatives to sell their products on a straight commission basis. Granted, there may be in fact individuals who earned six-figure incomes selling shower attachments, but their numbers are usually quite small. Retail chains also have problems attracting candidates since they suffer from the reputation of offering jobs with long hours and initially low pay. Some of these companies try to get potential candidates in the door through any means possible. They work under the assumption that the opportunity can be sold more effectively face to face. Unless you are specifically focussing on a straight commission or retail job, you don't want to spend valuable time interviewing for these opportunities.

How do you spot these ads? The term "management trainee," especially if the company or industry is not mentioned, often means a retail position. "Unlimited income opportunity" is a tip-off for a straight commission sales job. What they leave out is that there also isn't any income floor. You're free to earn as much or as little as you can. The more flowery or vague the language, the more cautious you should be. Look at companies seeking "dynamic self-starters who aren't afraid of a challenge" that don't provide any additional information about the job with a certain amount of skepticism. After all, what company wouldn't want to hire dynamic self-starters who aren't afraid of a challenge? The more puff surrounding the job description the more you want to consider whether it's a good investment of your time to investigate the position further.

A key strategy in answering ads is to identify the exact nature of the work as early as possible with a minimum investment of time. You can save a great deal of time by getting the pertinent information in an initial phone call rather than by the more time-consuming interview process. However, since some of the commission-only companies are most interested in getting you to show up in person, the information may not be readily forthcoming. A tip-off is if your phone call is answered by an individual who can only "schedule appointments." If the next step in the process is attendance at a seminar or meeting, you can virtually guarantee that you will be presented with the opportunity to sell something to someone and earn "unlimited income."

Although there are exceptions to everything, the larger the ad the better the potential opportunities. Large display ads in which the company is named and the opportunity is clearly spelled out represent the least amount of risk. Large display ads that refer you to a post office box are also usually worth pursuing if your background and interests match the requirements of the ad. However, as mentioned before, you should be cautious of "blind ads," lest you wind up applying to your own company.

CHAPTER 9

DEVELOPING
YOUR RÉSUMÉ

❧

Once you've focussed on the type of job you want and identified some prospective employers, it's time to prepare your résumé. Remember, the purpose of the résumé is to get your foot in the door. Ultimately, your job search is little more than an exercise in sales. You'll never be able to close the sale and receive an offer until you come face to face with your future boss. When putting together your résumé ask yourself, "If I were hiring someone for this job, what would I be looking for?" Your answer will tell you what to include and highlight.

The problem with proper résumé etiquette is not that there is too little advice; in fact the exact opposite is true. Everyone from your Aunt Zelda to your postal carrier has specific ideas of what should be included. Although their advice is well meaning, unless you're careful, you'll find yourself rewriting your résumé to conform to every suggestion you hear. While you don't want to do anything strange (such as putting a cartoon on your résumé), there is a variety of formats, all of which are effective and acceptable.

Chronological or Functional?

Use a chronological format unless there is something unusual about your background. This standard layout shows each job you've held, beginning with your most recent and working backward. It is the most commonly used résumé format and is suitable for most people.

An alternative format is the functional résumé. This format stresses either the types of jobs you've had or certain qualities you feel may be of interest to prospective employers. Functional résumés do not tie accomplishments to specific employers and are often designed to create what appears to be a progression of responsibilities. Since specific dates are not included, it is commonly used by those who have gaps in their employment history. Unfortunately, employers know this and tend to look at functional resumes with a great deal of skepticism.

Including an Objective

The objective should be no more than two sentences long and state specifically what you're applying for and why you're qualified. Unfortunately, many people do the exact opposite, writing desperate tomes:

> My goal is to secure a position that will allow me to develop a career which will make the most of my dreams and aspirations to become a valuable asset to a company that I would like to work for . . .

> To work within the management framework of a department that will provide maximum responsibilities with minimum limitations in the execution of those responsibilities with advancement to the highest level of management to be achieved by my abilities . . .

A superior job objective has two key components: what you want to do and what you can bring to the party. The following are good examples:

> Seeking a computer operator's position utilizing my five years experience in the design and test of PC-based software systems.

> Mechanical engineering position that would use my experience in vibration, rotor dynamics, and stress analysis.

> Nondestructive testing position that would utilize my experience in liquid penetrant and x-ray tests.

Never forget that the reader is asking themselves one question as they peruse your résumé, "Does this person have the skills to do what I need to have done?"

Designing Your Résumé

If you are a recent college graduate, put your education first, followed by full- or part-time work experience. If you are an experienced worker, put your work history first. Since résumés are initially only scanned briefly, you want to put the information of the most interest to the reader as close to the top of the résumé as possible.

Use bullet points and hanging indents to highlight the most important aspects of your background. Limit each paragraph to no more than eight lines of type. This will make your résumé pleasing to the eye and eliminate clutter. Leave at least a one-inch margin on each side of the paper.

White paper is the best color for your résumé since you'll want the paper for your cover letter to match. One woman prepared a beautiful résumé on light gray paper, but was continually searching for gray paper for her cover letters. The job search is difficult enough without placing additional minor hurdles in your way.

There's nothing magical about a one-page résumé; however, most experts agree that it should not exceed two pages. Devote the greatest amount of space to your most recent experience. Most employers are primarily interested in what you've been doing for the past ten years. You can summarize earlier experience by using statements such as, "Began my career as a forklift operator and subsequently was promoted though several supervisory positions."

Things to Leave Out

Don't include a photo or references on your résumé. It always seems like the strangest-looking people insist on including their photo. References won't be called until after you've been interviewed, so list them separately. You'll need four to six references who can discuss your work capabilities rather than attest to your fine moral fiber. Co-workers, former bosses, and other friends from work make the best references. Since most reference checks will be conducted by phone, make sure you ask your references if they prefer to be called at work or at home. (The etiquette of obtaining references is discussed in Chapter 10.)

Don't include the reasons you left previous employers. It's considered bad résumé etiquette to do so, and the reasons are better discussed face to face.

Leave off your spouse's name, how long you've been married (they're not hiring the two of you), and the names of your kids and/or their health. There is also no need to include a statement of your own health; it is assumed to be fine.

Don't put the word "Résumé" at the top of the page, and omit that pernicious tag line, "References will be provided upon request." Obviously you're going to give references if asked.

Emphasize Accomplishments

The key to a successful résumé is to focus on your accomplishments rather than your responsibilities. This is the most difficult part of preparing a résumé. After all, it's hard for many of us to remember what we were doing six months ago, much less years ago. This is why it's a good idea to update your résumé once a year, even if you're perfectly content in your job.

When listing your accomplishments, you'll want to use action verbs, such as "accomplished," "developed," "investigated," "managed," or "negotiated." Thinking about these words can also help you brainstorm about additional accomplishments you might have forgotten.

The more accomplishments you pack into your résumé, the greater the likelihood you'll get called in for an interview.

Using a Résumé Service

Out of frustration and anxiety many job seekers turn to résumé preparation services. Although these services sometimes can help, relying on them to develop your résumé from scratch is usually a bad idea.

Many people turn to services simply because they don't know what they should put on their résumé. The art of résumé writing is often shrouded in myth and lore, making inexperienced writers nervous. Actually, if you use your common sense, you'll do fine. Keep in mind that there is no such things as the "perfect" résumé. Everyone has a slightly different opinion about what a résumé should look like. Most experts agree that there is a range of acceptability; as long as yours falls within that range, you're fine.

You should always make a serious attempt to develop your own résumé before paying for professional help. No one knows your background as well as you. Résumé writers can help you communicate what you've done, but, unless you provide them with the basic data, you'll likely wind up with a document that doesn't truly reflect your capabilities.

Only after you've completed the initial steps in developing your résumé should you consider using a preparation service. The major benefits these firms provide are organization and editing. If you've had more than your fair share of jobs in the past ten years or are worried about how to condense 30 years of experience into two pages, a résumé writing service may be able to offer you good advice. However, make sure the finished product is an accurate reflection of your background. If an interviewer discovers one falsehood on your résumé, your chances of getting the job are slim to none.

A writing service can help you articulate your background and accomplishments. Although most firms also offer career counseling services, writing and editing capabilities are most important. Just because someone can help you identify specific career options does not necessarily mean they can effectively describe your skills on paper. Ask for examples of résumés they have produced in the past. Is the copy short and succinct? Does it capture your attention? Put yourself in a prospective employer's shoes. How would you react if you received this résumé? If your reaction is positive, the firm is worth considering further.

How do you find résumé writing services? Many firms advertise extensively in daily newspapers or the Yellow Pages. You can also check out the advisors section in the back of the book *What Color is Your Parachute?* Recent college graduates should expect to pay $65 to $100 for a one-page résumé. Experienced professionals need to budget $125 to $200. If your work experience is spotty, or if you are attempting to change fields completely, expect to pay more.

Although your résumé is an important component in your job search, its role is often overemphasized. Far too many candidates agonize that if only they had included one thing instead of another they would be gainfully employed. In reality, hiring criteria is complex and subjective. One line on a résumé seldom makes that much of a difference. Once you've completed your résumé, put it aside. Its easy to rationalize that the reason you're not getting offers is because of what's on your résumé, but this is seldom the case.

CHAPTER 10

USING REFERENCES

The managing partner of a large midwest law firm related the following unfortunate story to me. He received a telephone call one morning from the employment manager seeking to hire an in-house attorney. The employment manager said that the vice-president had been named as a reference by the individual. Would he be willing to discuss the circumstances under which he knew the candidate? Normally, the partner would have been delighted, except in this instance he could not recall who the individual was. The impression this left on the employment manager can well be imagined.

Not informing individuals that you are giving their names as references, or not prepping them on what you would like for them to say about you, is often an overlooked component of the job search campaign. Unfortunately, mishandling references can cause real problems that could otherwise be avoided. Although it seems obvious, many job seekers don't take the extra step of discussing their job search strategy with the people they intend to use as references. Doing so is well worth the effort. Let's examine how you can maintain control over the reference check process and use it to your maximum advantage.

How many references do you need? You should be prepared to provide four to six individuals who can speak about your professional, technical, or managerial capabilities. These might include supervisors, co-workers, vendors, or customers. They should all be prepared to speak about you from a business perspective. Individuals who can only attest to your fine moral fiber are of less interest to recruiters and interviewers.

If you are a recent college graduate with little work experience, teachers and professors are suitable alternatives to employers. However, try to include only those teachers who really know you. Recruiters will not be impressed with a professor whose only comment is, "According to my records, Tina received an A in my class."

Tread equally carefully in the use of celebrities or famous personalities. Recruiters look at these references with a great deal of skepticism. However, if you have established connections with individuals who are highly regarded in your particular industry, their recommendation can carry great weight and help you open doors.

An often overlooked, yet critical step in preparing your references on what you want them to say about you. First, you should discuss the type of job for which you are applying. Next, talk about those aspects of your previous experience that most relate to the requirements of the prospective assignment. Ask your reference if he or she feels comfortable discussing your background in a particular area. Give your reference examples of when you demonstrated a particular skill which you think would be of interest to the recruiter. In order to provide such examples you will have to extensively research the company and make educated assumptions about the skills for which it is looking. You are likely to be pleased when you learn the anecdotes your reference cited to the recruiter were the same ones discussed in your preparation meeting. Far too often job seekers leave this to chance.

Thank your references for the role they are playing in your job search and include them in your list of people receiving periodic updates on your job search effort. You will find that most people are flattered to be asked to serve as a reference and are very interested in the success of your job search. Don't forget to ask your references who else you should be contacting in your job search. These individuals are often invaluable networking contacts.

Your references may be asked to provide the names of other people who can speak about your skills. Discuss this with them in advance. Suggest names of other individuals that the reference might give if he or she is asked. It is important that you maintain control over the reference checking process.

Will your references be called? No precise information has been collected on this subject, yet anecdotal feedback from recruiters indicates that it is unlikely all provided references will be called. However it's impossible to predict which of your references will be contacted, so it's best to make sure all your references are prepared as we have discussed.

CHAPTER 11

INTERVIEWING

Unfortunately, most people just don't interview as well as they think they do. Job seekers confidently say, "If I can just get the interview, I'll be able to get the job," or "I've always done well once I've gotten the interview." However, these same individuals are likely to say after the interview, "Boy, I sure wasn't expecting some of those questions," or "I don't think it went very well."

The issue isn't that you're likely to completely botch the interview. Very few candidates actually do that. What's more common is not making much of an impression one way or the other. Since companies tend to interview a large number of applicants, your odds of becoming just another candidate are quite high. How can you break out of the pack and distinguish yourself in the interview? Keep these interviewing etiquette points in mind:

1. **Don't interview just for the sake of interviewing.** A lot of job seekers focus their initial efforts on obtaining interviews. Lots of interviews. It doesn't matter what type of job it is: "As long as I'm out interviewing, I must be making progress on my job search, right?" Wrong. Unless you truly believe you are well qualified for a position don't waste your time interviewing. Some people think going out on "practice interviews" will help them improve their interviewing skills. In reality, there's a world of difference between interviewing for a job you're interested in and one you don't care about. Before going out on any interview make sure you're convinced that it's worth your time. Be respectful of your own time and the time of whoever will have to interview you. Given the large number of truly qualified candidates, it's highly unlikely you'll be successful in bluffing your way into an offer. Think about what your skills are and what you're really interested in. If you're not sure, taking some vocational aptitude tests, such as the Strong or the Campbell Inventory, may be a good investment.

2. **Practice your answers.** Although it's impossible to prepare for every screwball question you might get asked, not having the basic questions down pat is an inexcusable interviewing sin. You can safely assume that 90 percent of interviewers are going to ask you one of the two most popular questions: "So, tell me a little about yourself," or "What are your strengths and weaknesses?" We'll talk more about the questions you need to be prepared for shortly. When you're practicing your answers, make sure you speak out loud. There's a world of difference between thinking to yourself what you'll say and actually articulating the answer. Like everything else in life, your answers will be smoother and more persuasive the more you practice.

3. **Ask good questions.** I'm always surprised that interviewees don't realize that the questions they ask are just as important as the answers they give. Otherwise savvy job seekers will spend hours preparing for the common question and not give two seconds of thought to the questions they should ask. As a result they miss a golden opportunity to both learn more about the job and improve their standing in the eye of the interviewer. Candidates are often uncertain about what types of questions to ask. Focus on questions that will give you insights into what it's like to work for the company or the criteria for career success. While the company is not likely to voluntarily tell you the incumbent was fired, you can find out if you ask what happened to the person who had the job previously. You'll be surprised at how much you can learn if only you remember to ask the right questions.

Too often candidates try to play it safe and ask only puffball questions lest they offend the interviewer. By all means, don't ask about benefits in the initial interview. While benefits are important, asking this question in the initial round is considered one of the all time "dumb" questions among experienced interviewers. While you never want to be rude, don't pass up this opportunity to investigate whether the job is truly right for you. For example, if the company puts a great emphasis on team work and you know that you prefer to work alone, the time to find this out is before accepting the job, not afterwards. Remember, the goal of the job search is not to get the most offers—just the right one.

Improving Your Odds

So, how can you improve your odds of making a good impression? You may be surprised to learn that developing the gift of storytelling can be a very powerful weapon. Using stories to describe your accomplishments helps you stand out and be remembered. The reason for this has to do with one of the basic premises of adult education. Adults tend to remember examples better than they remember facts. If you list off a string of strengths, such as resourceful, articulate, and pleasant, no one will remember what you said 15 minutes after you leave the interview. Moreover, by simply articulating a laundry list of strengths you are not backing up your claim. Maybe these really are strengths, but who knows? By describing situations in which you demonstrated those strengths, you will both convince the interviewer that these are indeed strengths, and you will have a higher probability of being remembered after the interview is over.

Telling stories about your background is a skill. Some people are naturally good at it, others are not. However, it is a skill that most people can master with a little practice. The trick is to establish a format for your anecdotes. This will enable you to avoid being too brief or overly long-winded. The acronym STAR is often helpful in providing this framework:

- First, think about a *situation* or *task* that you faced. Describe this situation in two or three sentences. This establishes the background for your story so the recruiter can understand it.

- Next, describe the *action* you took. At this stage, it is important that you speak specifically about what you did. There is a tendency for candidates to gloss over their accomplishments and hide their light under the proverbial bushel. While you don't want to appear arrogant, you do want to take credit for the role that you played.

- Conclude your anecdote by describing the *result* you achieved. Discuss how your work helped your employer. Whenever possible try to discuss results in measurable or quantifiable terms.

For example, an accountant described a time in which an accounting system he was expected to implement quickly was threatened by a manager who was slow to commit his support. To convince the manager to support the effort, the accountant proposed a 7:00 A.M. meeting to discuss the project. Both the presentation and the accountant's willingness to meet so early impressed the manager, who gave his approval. The accounting system was then quickly implemented. As a result, the system decreased the time it took to process invoices by 25 percent.

Pretend you are an interviewer who just heard the anecdote from the accountant. You probably associate the accountant with such positive traits as initiative, hard working, detail oriented, and resourceful. Additionally, you would likely remember this anecdote and the accountant for some time to come. It is easy to see why using stories in the interview is such a powerful weapon.

Identifying the right stories to tell is a critical step. You will want to prepare an array of anecdotes that can be deployed as needed during the interview. The first step is to compile a list of situations or activities in which you have been successful in the past. These can relate to work, school, or other outside interests. You should be able to come up with an initial list of at least 30 situations. For each of these, write out the corresponding action you took and the result you achieved. Don't worry if you can't quantify all of your results. Although it makes for a more impressive story if you can, sometimes the results is simply that the project was completed on time.

A final step before the interview is to put yourself in the interviewer's shoes. If you were hiring someone for this job what types of skills would you be looking for? Write them down. Review your list of anecdotes to identify which stories demonstrate your skills in those areas. By preparing and articulating your anecdotes, you will find that you will be remembered positively while your competition becomes a blur in the recruiter's mind.

Handling Common Questions

Although Woody Allen once said that 90 percent of life was just showing up, success in an interview depends on more than just arriving on time. While no two interviews are exactly the same, certain questions are asked frequently. I still feel my blood pressure rise when I remember my first interview. I stayed up the better part of the night reviewing the class notes from every course I'd taken since high school. I prepared succinct, concise answers about how each class played some important role in preparing me for the job for which I was interviewing. I even figured out a way to impress, at least myself, with the awesome responsibilities I had had during the past summer as an assistant evening front desk manager at the Waltham Motor Inn.

When the interviewer, Mr. Wilson, resplendent in a lime green polyester suit, came to greet me in the reception area, I immediately noticed his resemblance to Wally Cox. "This is going to be a piece of cake," I smugly told myself as I took a seat in the interview room.

"So, Mark, tell me a little bit about yourself," said Mr. Wilson. Suddenly, the term "drawing a blank" took on new meaning for me. Amid numerous "ums" and "ahhs," I somehow got the answer out with the predictable amount of impressiveness. I think my rejection letter was waiting for me by the time I got home.

Some of the toughest common questions include the following:

- **Tell me about yourself.** This question is difficult precisely because it's so broad. You can try to throw it back at the interviewer, but that strategy seldom works. If you say, "What exactly would you like to know?" the interviewer will respond, "Oh, I don't care, just tell me a little bit about yourself." The best strategy for dealing with this question is as follows:

1. One or two sentences about background, family, and so on: "Well, I'm originally from Montana. Mom's an astronaut and Dad's a beekeeper. I'm the youngest of seven."

2. Transition into the aspect of your background that you think most closely matches the requirements of the job: "As you can see on my résumé, I've spent the past two years selling Wimpy Widgets to a client base similar to yours." You can elaborate from here on how your experience meets the needs of the company, but try to keep your answer to no more than three minutes.

- **What are your strengths and weaknesses?** Obviously it is much easier to answer the first part of this question. However, make sure that you provide a specific example to back up your claim. Anyone can say that dealing with people under pressure is a strength. By providing a concrete example of when you demonstrated this skill, you will convince the interviewer that this is truly one of your assets. Talking about a weakness will not hurt your candidacy as long as you also discuss the steps you are taking to improve this area. Discuss a weakness that is both common and correctable, such as giving a speech: "One of the areas my boss mentioned I needed to work on is making a presentation before a group. To improve in this area, I enrolled in the Toastmasters Presentation Workshop and actively sought out opportunities to speak before groups. Although today I'm not someone who's considering going on the Broadway stage, I do feel that I am able to express myself persuasively and concisely."

- **What's your opinion of your co-workers?** This question is often asked to see if the interviewers can get you to speak negatively about your business associates. They figure that if they can get you to speak badly about co-workers, you're likely to be a negative influence on the workforce. Thus, regardless of your personal opinion of your fellow workers, mention only their positive attributes. Remember that the interview is a sales situation and not a confessional. Always speak from the positive side and eliminate the negative.

- **Who was the boss you had the most difficulty working with?** Again, the attempt is being made to get you to speak negatively about an individual. If you talk about the differences in opinion or clashes in management style you had with your boss, you'll come across as defensive. Answer this question by articulating what you learned from the experience. If you can discuss how you grew as an employee as a result of working for the individual, you'll greatly impress the interviewer.

- **How many hours a week do you have to work in order to accomplish your job?** Be careful here. Candidates sometimes trip themselves up by stating that they work an excessive number of hours. Unfortunately, this can leave the impression that if only you worked more efficiently you would accomplish more. An effective method by which to answer this question is to approach it from the standpoint that one's job is never truly complete: "Given the nature of my work, it's possible that I could devote every waking hour to the job and still have opportunities left unexplored. I think what is important is knowing how to focus on the important issues and not get overly involved in the minutia associated with a project. I find that to a certain extent I never really completely turn off my thinking about work since I often get good ideas about how to grow the business at all sorts of different times."

- **How long will you stay with us?** Obviously, the company is looking for a level of commitment and will avoid recruiting obvious job hoppers. However, going overboard and committing yourself as an indentured servant is both silly and most likely unbelievable. In answering this question, focus on the challenge of the assignment: "One of the things that attracted me to this company is that I feel this assignment will provide me with a lot of professional challenge. Feeling that I am contributing to the growth of the organization is very important to me. As long as I remain challenged, I would not anticipate having the desire to seek employment elsewhere."

- **Are you willing to relocate?** If you are interviewing for a branch office assignment, this question is often asked to determine if you are willing to eventually relocate to the company's headquarters. This is an issue for companies such as Nike, where all roads eventually lead to Oregon. Other times the question is asked to determine your willingness to make sacrifices in the company's interest. In preparation for this question, research where the company's headquarters and major facilities are.

- **What aspects of your job do you consider the most critical?** Usually asked to determine your ability to differentiate the important from the mundane. Answer this question by focusing on those aspects that either help build the business or contribute to the bottom line. There is a compelling business reason why you were hired to do your job. Articulate those critical components.

Keep in mind that there are often multiple agenda items associated with otherwise straightforward-seeming questions. Think through what you think the interviewer is really trying to get at and answer accordingly.

Asking Your Own Questions

"Well, I guess that takes care of the questions I had for you. Now, tell me, what would you like to know?" Recruiters are often amazed that otherwise well-prepared, highly talented candidates leave their common sense at home when it comes time for them to ask questions in the interview. The inability to ask meaningful questions can kill an otherwise successful interview.

Unfortunately, most individuals emphasize how to answer the most commonly asked questions. As a result, many of them are at a loss as to what additional questions to ask, and more importantly, what questions not to raise. Knowing the etiquette of what to ask in the interview can dramatically improve your chances of getting the offer.

The most serious mistake applicants make is not having questions prepared for each individual interviewer. Candidates often compound this mistake by then saying, "No, I don't think I have any questions that you could answer," or "I think I'll wait till I meet the hiring manager before I ask my questions." Put yourself in the interviewer's shoes. How would you feel if an applicant said either of these things to you? Insulted? Belittled? It hardly makes you want to rush out and hire the person. Remember, hiring is usually a consensus decision. The supervising manager will seek support for his or her decision from the other interviewers. Slighting any of the interviewers will only reduce your odds of receiving an employment offer.

Asking a "nonquestion" also represents a significant missed opportunity. Everyone in the interviewing process has a unique perspective on the company, the position, and what it's like working for the firm. Some interviewers have a "big picture" perspective, whereas others have an intimate, detailed knowledge on the specific functions of the job. You need to understand these different perspectives and develop appropriate questions. A helpful tool in preparing questions is to obtain a list of who will be on the interview schedule as early as possible. Then you can prepare questions that take advantage of the individual perspectives of these different managers.

A common question many job seekers have is whether it's appropriate for an applicant to bring a list of prepared questions to the interview. The overall interview presentation is stronger when a candidate asks questions without referring to notes. However, the interview is a high-pressure situation and under such circumstances even the best-prepared applicants may forget what it was they wanted to ask. Thus, bring your list of questions with you to the interview, but only refer to it if you temporarily forget your questions. In fact, having the questions available as a backup tends to make you more relaxed and actually reduces the odds of you're having to refer to them.

It is not a sin to ask the same question of more than one interviewer. Candidates sometimes feel that once a question has been asked it may not be repeated. Actually, there is an advantage to asking similar questions of different interviewers. This allows you to gauge the consistency of opinions within the organization.

Be careful not to overdo the questioning or ask about obscure information. Although researching a company is important, some candidates seem to take a perverse delight in asking a question the interviewer can't answer. Once when I was recruiting a marketing assistant for a large cheese manufacturing company, the candidate asked about the role that hydroponics would play in the corporation's future plans. I wasn't certain I knew what hydroponics were, much less what role they played in the cheese business. It did turn out that a small division of the company, not associated with the cheese business, was experimenting with growing plants in nontraditional environments. Unfortunately for the candidate, my opinion of him dwindled. Of all the questions he could have asked, he chose a question notable only for its obscurity. In asking a question solely to see if you can trip up the interviewer, you may win the battle and lose the war.

It's sometimes hard to believe that applicants still ask about salaries and benefits in their initial questions. Although these are important subjects, they should not be raised in the first round of questions. They give the interviewer the distinct impression that you are more interested in dollars and cents than challenge and opportunity. Opinions vary somewhat on the subject, so the best strategy is to let the interviewer raise the subject of compensation.

Good Questions to Ask

So, what should you be asking in the interview? It's helpful to prepare both "micro" and "macro" questions. That is, questions that focus both on the specifics of the job, as well as more general questions about the overall company and industry.

Good questions pertain to the job and indicate your interest in obtaining information important in making a career decision. Think hard about what you really need to know in order to evaluate your career potential with a company. For example, questions such as "How will my performance be evaluated?'' or ''What is the management style of the company?'' give you information you can use to evaluate the organization.

You also might consider asking questions such as ''Can you tell me about the top five duties of this position?'' or ''What would you expect me to accomplish in the first four weeks on the job?'' Both of these questions are excellent in helping you determine the exact nature of the job and your supervisor's demands.

Although your turn to ask questions will generally occur toward the end of the interview, if you have the chance to ask questions early, you can use it to your advantage. For example, we've discussed the most common questions used by interviewers, including, ''Tell me about yourself.'' After you've answered this question, end your answer with a question of your own, such as ''Tell me, what are you looking for in a candidate?'' Obtaining this information early allows you to focus on those aspects of your background that most closely meet the needs of the employer. It's amazing how much information you can get about the company and the job if you only remember to ask.

Other good questions include those that make the interviewer think. This is especially important when you're interviewing with a human resources representative. These people do a lot of interviewing, and it can get boring being asked the same old questions over and over again. Two questions that fall outside the norm include the following:

- ''If I surveyed the people who worked here and asked them what they liked most about the company and, conversely, what frustrates them, what do you think I would hear?'' This question gives you a lot of valuable information that will help you determine whether you would fit in well with the company. Secondly, this question is particularly effective with human resources managers because these are the issues they deal with from day to day. The human resources interviewer can often give you some valuable insights into these important issues.

- ''When you look at the people who have been successful here, what tend to be their strengths? Are there any common characteristics among people who don't work out?'' This question will give you information about what characteristics and skills are important for success with this company. For example, if you learn that people who succeed are those who can work effectively in teams, and you know that in your heart of hearts you're a lone ranger working best as an individual contributor, the odds of your being happy and successful are rather slim.

- ''How will you and I know that I am successful in this job?'' Along with knowing what it takes to be successful, you'll also want to know how you'll be evaluated. Don't forget to ask.

- "What are some of the competitive challenges the company currently faces?" or "Have there been any recent reorganizations or layoffs?" In addition to information about the specific job, you'll also want to find out about the overall health of the company. While you may not feel entirely comfortable asking these questions, this is information you need to know before accepting an offer.

- "What's the next step, where do we go from here?" Make a note of when the company told you they would be back in contact and don't be shy about following up if you don't hear back. This is a nice way to end the interview.

Excellent questions make interviewers think. They probe beyond the superficial and zero in on key issues that can affect the job or the company. Strive to develop some unique relevant questions for your next interview. Most candidates don't fully realize how much they are judged by the questions they ask. Those who do have a competitive advantage.

Explaining an Extended Absence from the Workforce

Mildred has been out of the workforce for the past ten years, devoting herself to raising her two sons. Although she has a master's degree, she is finding it difficult to obtain new employment.

Saul suffered multiple injuries from a serious car accident. Now fully recovered, he's uncomfortable drawing attention to his period of recuperation, yet is uncertain about how to explain the time away from work.

These are but two examples of the many people who struggle to explain extended absences from full-time work. While the job search is difficult enough for anyone, unfortunately, a prolonged absence makes re-entering the workforce even more challenging. You may find that you can't pick up exactly where you left off. You may have to take the proverbial "one step backward, to take two steps forward." Although this doesn't mean that you should needlessly compromise your career objectives, it is important that you set realistic and obtainable goals.

Although you're ultimately going to have to account for your time away from work, you want to be careful about how you communicate this information. It's a lot easier to explain extended absences face to face than on paper. Thus, you may be able to increase your odds of getting an interview by using a non-traditional résumé format. Although the chronological résumé, which presents your background in reverse chronological order, is the most common form of résumé, it also highlights any time you've been away from work. Consider the functional résumé as an alternative. Functional résumés focus on what you've done rather than when you did it. To prepare a functional résumé, identify three or four areas in which you have specific expertise. These might include management, technical skills, training, data processing and so on. For each category, list your specific accomplishments and achievements. Don't worry about when the actual accomplishment occurred. The impression you want to convey for each category is that you've had specific experience and a track record of success.

Toward the bottom of your functional résumé, list the companies for which you've worked and the positions you've held. Omitting months and including only years of employment can sometimes help in minimizing the appearance of time off. While a functional résumé can help disguise your time away from the work environment, some employers view the format with skepticism. However, it can help open several doors that might otherwise remain closed.

Once you're in the interview you need to be prepared for three questions:

1. Why did you take the time off?

2. What did you accomplish or learn that would be of benefit to a prospective employer?

3. Why do you want to re-enter the employment marketplace?

If you can state practical reasons for doing what you did, you should be able to overcome a prospective employer's concerns.

It's very important that you avoid being defensive concerning your absence from the workforce. Dwelling on the issue only creates more concerns. Try to focus your answers on work-related accomplishments. Of course, you're going to have to account for the time, so prepare a brief answer that explains why you took time off and why you're now seeking full-time employment. As with all interview questions, the more you practice this answer out loud prior to the interview, the more confident you'll be.

If the reason for your absence was health related, this issue is often difficult to handle in an interview. Technically employers can't ask you about medical issues aside from questions such as "This job requires the ability to lift a 25-pound box; can you perform that task?" However, you may want to take a more proactive approach to address any perceived concerns. Some people decide that the best course of action is to raise the issue themselves: "As you can see on my résumé, I've been out of the workforce since 1992. Unfortunately, I was in a severe car accident and required an extended period of recovery. However, my doctors now say I'm fine, and I'm looking forward to getting back to work full-time."

Although re-entering the workforce isn't easy, it is possible. By using a résumé format that doesn't draw attention to your time away from work, candidly discussing the reasons for your absence, and persuasively articulating your work-related accomplishment, you can beat the odds.

Dealing with the Overqualification Issue

Remember those initial Catch-22 job search frustrations? You needed experience to get a job, yet how did you get the experience? Ironically, an increasing number of job seekers are experiencing the corollary to this dilemma; they have too much experience for the position for which they are applying. Although there are a number of valid reasons individuals apply for positions for which they are overqualified, employers remain highly skeptical about hiring such people.

These concerns about hiring an overqualified candidate are often justified. Will the individual really be committed to staying on the job, or is he or she just looking for a position to last until something better comes along? Will the person find a job with reduced responsibilities stimulating after six months? Is he or she really willing to take the pay reduction these positions usually require?

Many employers have been burned by candidates whose job tenure was brief despite interview commitments to the contrary. You have to remember that hiring is a time-consuming, expensive, and arduous task. Once the person has finally been hired, the employer's major concern is that he or she will quit, thus necessitating that the hiring process begin all over again. Thus, the overqualified candidate represents some valid risks which must be carefully handled if they are to be overcome.

The first step is to seriously evaluate your reasons for accepting a position with reduced responsibility. Blanca Rohr, a consultant with the outplacement form of Drake Beam & Morin, says that it is important to evaluate your career objectives. Some individuals set their sights too low and are primarily motivated by the goal of finding a job—any job—as quickly as possible. While becoming unemployed is often a scary experience, you should spend the time necessary to determine exactly what you are looking for in a position. Make sure you are realistic in your expectations, but don't sell yourself short.

Certainly, there are very valid reasons for accepting a position for which you may be overqualified. A desire for more time to spend with family or an interest in becoming more involved in community activities may indicate that such a job makes good sense. Technically trained individuals are often interested in returning to an individual contributor's role and forgoing the time commitments and administrative headaches a managerial position often involves. Ms. Rohr points out that the key lesson is to carefully think through your own individual situation and not be too quick to compromise on your career potential.

Interviewing for a position that represents a reduction in responsibilities presents its own unique challenges. Lewis Kravitz, with the outplacement firm Right Associates, indicate that interview success is highly dependent on focussing on your prior accomplishments and achievements, rather than discussing the scope of responsibilities in your most current assignment. Communicate the philosophy that your additional experience only enhances the value you will be able to bring to the job.

Addressing the Issue

Statements such as "When I look back on my career, I realize I was happiest when I was performing this particular type of work," can help reduce an employer's fears. Emphasize the match between your skills and the employer's needs. Give specific examples about how you handled similar tasks in earlier assignments. Convey lots of enthusiasm about the type of work you performed.

If you are seeking a job for which you are technically overqualified, you may find that the standard chronological résumé does not serve your needs. Chronological résumés that emphasize career advancement and progression may reinforce concerns among potential employers. A functional résumé, highlighting technical skills and specific accomplishments, may be of greater benefit.

You also would be well advised to think through compensation issues carefully before accepting a position with reduced responsibility. Be prepared for a reduction in pay. Although candidates often articulate a willingness to accept a lower salary in the interview, once the financial repercussions of their decision become apparent, a severe case of buyer's remorse sets in. You should take a hard look at your financial commitments and determine what type of pay cut you can realistically afford to take.

The key lesson to remember if you are considering accepting a position with reduced responsibilities is to first make sure you are taking a position for the right reasons and not selling yourself short.

Negotiating Salary

Perhaps no other interview question causes as much anxiety as, "So, tell me what type of salary you're looking for." What are you supposed to say?

Should you quote a precise figure? Talk in broad ranges? Plead indifference? Respond humorously? What exactly are you worth?

Not knowing your market value is a huge obstacle in the salary negotiation process. The results of not knowing what you're worth can be disastrous. If you ask for $30,000 but the company was willing to go $35,000, it's unlikely they will pay you the extra $5,000 simply out of the goodness of their heart.

Ideally, the subject of salaries will be left to the end of the interview. This is ideal, but not realistic. The question may be the first one out of the interviewer's mouth or the last. Although there is no way to predict when the subject will be raised, you can rest assured it will come up. You may be asked about your salary needs on the employment application. This is especially true if you're applying for an entry-level position. As much as the employer would like you to name your price, doing so is not in your best interests. Write in "negotiable," "open," or "will discuss."

A common request in newspaper help wanted ads is for candidates to include their salary requirements. Some ads even go on to state, "No applications will be considered without salary information." This is really a lot of hogwash. No one in their right mind is going to rule you out solely because you didn't include this information. If they do, they are probably not the type of people you would want to go to work for anyway.

Keep in mind that the "What kind of money do you want?" question covers multiple agendas. While the interviewer wants to know your price, he or she also want to know which is more important to you—money or the job? The key is to strike a balance with your answer. You're primarily interested in the opportunity but expect to be paid a very competitive wage. For example, you may answer, "Well Mr. Sports Marketer, like everyone else I want to make as much money as I can. However, I'm mostly excited about the opportunity to develop a new golf tournament. From what you've told me, it seems that my background is a good match for what needs to be done."

At this stage you can try to turn the tables on the interviewer and find out how much he or she is willing to pay by asking, "What kind of money do you have budgeted for this position?" The key word here is "budgeted." Discussing the salary as simply a budgeted chunk of money, not dissimilar to office supplies, can sometimes cause the interviewer to tip his or her hand. ("We were thinking of bringing someone in between $45,000 to $50,000.")

A moment ago you may have been perfectly happy with $45,000. Now you realize there is more money on the table than you originally thought. You can maximize your position by bracketing the higher end of the quoted figure: "That would seem fair. I've been exploring opportunities in the $49,000 to $54,000 range."

This tactic tends to work better on line managers than it does the human resources recruiters. Line managers typically have less experience interviewing than personnel staff do, and they have a greater tendency to think in terms of budgeted numbers. While this tactic is worth trying, don't be surprised if your request for budgeted salary information is politely deflected with something like, "I'm not sure. It will depend on the individual. So, tell me, what type of money are you looking for?"

Ultimately, you've got to be prepared to talk about salary. You can determine what your market value is by talking with consultants in your industry or the placement director where you went to school. Based on the research you've conducted, mention a salary range rather than a specific number. Make sure your range is reasonable. Saying, "I'm looking at opportunities that pay from $35,000 to $80,000," will only make you look silly. A range of $5,000 to $10,000 is appropriate for most people. Make sure you do your homework before you go into the interview. Then you can handle the salary question to your best advantage.

Should you accept a lower salary in a new position? This is an issue confronting more and more job changers. There are no simple answers since each person's case is unique, but outplacement consultants and career change advisors state that there are compelling reasons both for and against accepting a lower salary.

Making the right salary decision depends on first knowing your market value. There are a number of methods to determine this. Co-workers are often a valuable source of information, although it is important to differentiate between what your co-workers think they should be making and true market value. Two more impartial sources are executive recruiting firms and university placement offices. Since executive recruiters earn their livelihood by keeping their fingers on the pulse of the employment marketplace, they are a particularly valuable resource. When discussing your compensation with a recruiter, make sure you are speaking with an individual who specializes in your field. Some of the larger firms, such as accounting recruiter Robert Half Inc., periodically publish salary surveys which are available on request.

Accepting a lower salary may be inevitable if you are a victim of a layoff from a large corporation. The salary scales for larger companies are often considerably higher than those for smaller employers. If you are restricted geographically and smaller employers are your most likely source of future employment, a lower salary is, unfortunately, a possible outcome.

The decision to accept a lower salary often makes sense if you are changing careers. In most cases, compensation directly relates to the amount of experience you have in a particular field. Walking away from your "career equity" by changing careers will normally result in your being paid less money. The reality of a lower salary is the ultimate test on how committed you are to changing professions. For some people, this financial sacrifice is worth it.

Finally, accepting a lower salary makes sense in situations where you can receive some other additional form of compensation. An example might be to take a smaller salary in exchange for an equity or ownership opportunity with a new employer. Individuals pursuing sales or marketing positions often work for a small base salary but have the potential to earn substantial total compensation through bonuses and commissions. If you are considering such an opportunity, make sure you fully understand how the bonuses are computed and how much individuals with backgrounds similar to yours have earned in their first year.

It seldom makes sense to accept less money if you are currently employed and being actively recruited by another company. If you are in this enviable position, you can expect the competing firm to make it worth your while to change jobs. Keep in mind that you are in a strong negotiating position, and it seldom pays to compromise too early. In fact, compromising too early on salary is one of the major sources of ultimate frustration for many job changers. While you should not have unrealistic salary expectations and compromise is a common element to the salary negotiation process, candidates often sell themselves short. This is particularly true of individuals who have been affected by a layoff. Since being laid off can greatly impact your self-esteem, an unfortunate reaction is to settle for less money than you can legitimately command in the marketplace. In these situations, as you settle into the new job and the financial compromise becomes economic reality, a great deal of job dissatisfaction can result. This often ultimately affects job performance and can prove disastrous.

Interestingly, there is a considerable amount of logic to support the contention that most employers will not intentionally cheat you on salary. The reason is that recruiting and hiring is an enormously time-consuming and expensive task. Once the arduous work of interviewing has been completed, the employer's greatest fear is that you will quit. Offering you a salary that is considerably below the current market is an invitation for employee turnover, which is often facilitated by a headhunter.

The key to determining what salary is right for you depends on first knowing your market value. Be realistic, but don't compromise too quickly. Only you can determine if it makes good sense to accept a lower salary in a new assignment.

Other Types of Compensation

Although salary is seldom the primary reason for accepting a position, it certainly is of considerable importance. However, salary is only one component of the total compensation package. When you receive an offer of employment you should investigate the following:

- **Performance bonus.** Participating in the company's bonus plan is one of the more common means of which you can increase your total compensation. Bonuses are usually based on a combination of factors, including overall company performance, your specific business unit's performance and your individual performance. Bonuses are typically a percentage of your base salary and can range from 10 percent to 100 percent. In larger organizations, participation in the bonus pool is largely determined by management level and may not be negotiable. However, in smaller companies that do not have a rigid policy on who may receive a bonus, this may be a subject worth negotiating.

- **Stock options.** Options enable you to acquire a specified number of shares at a preestablished price within a specific (usually ten-year) time frame. Historically, stock options were not only granted to individuals at very senior levels in an organization, but this has changed dramatically in recent years. For example, PepsiCo recently introduced a program in which all employees receive stock. Since stock options have the potential of being highly lucrative, you should consider discussing them in the salary negotiation process.

- **Signing bonuses.** One of the issues companies face in recruiting management talent is salary compression. It is difficult for a company to justify paying you more than they are paying existing employees performing a similar job. In order to attract highly qualified candidates, many companies offer a signing bonus. This enables you to achieve your compensation objectives without upsetting the existing salary structure.

- **Relocation allowance.** If your new job requires moving to a new location make sure you thoroughly investigate the relocation program. This is an often overlooked element of the compensation plan. At a minimum, most companies will provide for the physical move, such as loading furniture and delivering it to your new location. Additional issues you may want to negotiate include: increased insurance coverage on your transported furniture; a house-hunting trip to become familiar with the new location; temporary living accommodations and coverage of expenses while you make the transition to your new house; and a cash relocation allowance. These allowances are provided to cover relocation expenses, such as deposits for the telephone, gas, and electric companies. The amounts vary widely. Typically, renters are offered a sum equal to two weeks' salary, whereas home owners receive one month's salary. The actual amount is open to negotiation, so it pays to investigate.

- **Accelerated reviews.** If the salary offer is low but you are very excited about the opportunity, ask for an accelerated review date. Typically employees are reviewed and their salaries adjusted on an annual basis.

However, companies are often willing to review your performance in 90 days or six months. This gives you an opportunity to increase your salary based on a demonstration of your capabilities.

- **Benefits.** A company's benefit program is one of the least negotiable items in the total compensation package. As benefits are becoming increasingly expensive, the difference between corporate benefit programs have diminished significantly. Most benefit programs require you to participate in paying a percentage of the cost. Although the cost to you is significantly less than if you were to purchase the insurance on your own, it is still a substantial sum. Pay particular attention to companies offering "cafeteria" benefit programs. This form of benefits allows you to choose among an array of services. You can individualize a program that best meets the needs of yourself and your family.

As we have seen, total compensation is more than just the base salary you receive. By discussing these areas with your prospective employer, you may be able to increase the value of your total financial package.

Different Types of Interviewers

Susan thought she had prepared for everything. She had researched the company and practiced her answers to the most likely questions. She knew about the company's culture and could articulate why she would fit well with the company. With 15 years of related experience in the industry, Susan was the epitome of the confident candidate—until the interview started. "I was expecting to be interviewed by someone at least my own age, if not older. I also thought that I would most likely be interviewing with a man. When my prospective boss turned out to be a woman ten years younger than me, I was really surprised. She had a really strong New York accent which I'm not accustomed to. Although I tried to maintain my composure, I'm positive that my biases showed. I'm really not sure how well I did."

Being interviewed by someone significantly younger than you or from a different culture is increasingly common. In days gone by, you could safely assume your boss would be older than you. This was true because promotions within many major corporations were largely determined by how long you had worked for the company. It was also likely that your boss would be a white male. This has changed dramatically in a relatively short period of time. Some businesses, such as advertising, are often referred to as "young" industries. For example, 40-year-old employees are often supervised by managers in their twenties.

Although much has been written in the business press about diversity in the workforce, interviewing with someone of a different generation, sex, or culture can pose its own unique challenges. Thoughts such as "I've put in 15 years in this field. What can this person barely out of school know about this job?" are common. The issue isn't limited to applicants. Many employers also make snap judgments about candidates based on how different they appear or sound. The unfortunate consequence is that the person most similar to the interviewer, rather than the person best qualified for the job, often gets hired.

Even relatively superficial differences, such as your accent, can have a dramatic impact on how you are perceived. Southerners often think Northerners are rude, abrasive or, arrogant based largely on accents. Conversely, some Northerners perceive a female Southern accent as "cute." Southern men are often perceived by non-Southerners as "dumb" or "hicks" if they have a heavy Southern accent. It's simply not enough that we articulate our accomplishments and achievements. We have to be increasingly openminded about how such information is communicated and acknowledge differences in backgrounds. This is easier said than done.

These issues are a challenge for both employers and applicants alike. Candidates like Susan may become rattled when faced with a prospective manager who is different than what they expected. Consequently, they don't perform as well as they might in the interview. Employers may latch on to superficial differences and fail to fully explore a candidate's potential. Both sides lose if the right person isn't hired for these reasons.

What's the solution? How can candidates and employers overcome biases and concerns about someone who is "different" than they are? The answer isn't simple. "While there are no clear and obvious solutions," says Dr. Carol Beavers, senior vice-president with the outplacement firm EnterChange, "it is ultimately the responsibility of the candidate to recognize the barriers these differences in culture or speaking patterns may create." For example, if the interviewer speaks slowly, Dr. Beavers recommends that you pace your own speech accordingly. "When we are comfortable in a conversation, we find that we unconsciously start to mimic each other's behavior." Thus, the New Yorker who is interviewing with a Southerner may need to make a specific effort to slow down the pace at which he or she is speaking.

If you find yourself interviewing with someone considerably younger, Dr. Beavers recommends that you concentrate on your most recent work experiences rather than your first job out of school. For example, don't emphasize the differences in your age by mentioning such things as where you were employed when Kennedy was killed.

One of the problems with much of the advice on interviewing is that it assumes all interviewers are the same. As anyone who has spent any time in the interview trenches knows, nothing is further from the truth.

Interviewers vary enormously in style and level of competence. The gamut runs from managers who will talk endlessly about their companies and never allow you the opportunity to get a word in edgewise to interviewers who sit in stoic silence and barely say a word.

If you want to be successful you've got to be flexible in your interviewing style. Flexibility is one of the often overlooked keys to interview success. An interviewing style that may be highly effective with one type of interviewer may be completely ineffective with another. Unfortunately, some candidates naively believe that they should be hired solely on the merits of their background. The refuse to acknowledge that *how* they communicate is even more important than *what* they communicate. Yes, in the perfect society everyone would be hired solely on their accomplishments and achievements. The process would be completely fair. It would also have to be administered by computers because when humans are involved, a variety of outright biases often plays a major role in the decision. You can be morally right and unemployed, or you can adapt your interviewing style to the personality of the interviewer and hopefully achieve a more positive tangible result.

How interviewers decorate their office can tip you off about their interviewing style. For example, if there are lots of pictures of the company sports teams on display, you can assume that the interviewer values competitiveness and team players. If the credenza is filled with family pictures, the interviewer is apt to view the company as an extension of the family. In both of these cases, being perceived as a team player is likely to be quite important. You'll want to use the word "We" rather than "I" when articulating your accomplishments. Conversely, if the office has pictures of the manager engaged in individual competitive activities, such as tennis or golf, you'll want to emphasize the specific role you played in projects and activities.

Flexibility and adaptability are often overlooked components to interview success. By being aware of differences in styles, you can increase your likelihood of positively impressing a greater range of interviewers.

Handling a Bad Interviewer

One interviewer sits stoically behind the desk refusing to say a single word. Another interviewer talks endlessly about the job he or she has open but never asks you a question. Yet another latches on to some obscure, non–job-related aspect of your background and asks endless questions about it. As if interviewing weren't tough enough, running across an inept interviewer can make the process all the more arduous.

Unfortunately, your odds of running into these people is fairly high. It's not that they're malicious of spiteful—fortunately, the days of the "stress interviewer" are mostly behind us—rather they're usually either inexperienced or extremely uncomfortable with the interviewing process. Although you can never be completely prepared for every sort of off-the-wall interviewer, there are some recurring types with whom you should be prepared to deal.

First are the interviewers who have neither read your résumé nor have the slightest idea of what they should be asking you. Since this type of interviewer hasn't the foggiest notion of what to do, they are desperately hoping you will help them out and initiate the dialogue. While you don't want to be overly aggressive, if, after a reasonable time, no questions are forthcoming, you need to be prepared to begin the discussion.

Develop an opening statement to get the ball rolling: "I was really glad to have this opportunity to meet with you to discuss the production supervisor's job. I thought my background in supervision at Allied Chemical might be a good fit with your needs." Follow up by discussing those aspects of your background that most closely relate to the requirements of the position. For this strategy to be successful, you must have a clear understanding of exactly what the interviewer is looking for. The best way to prepare is to put yourself in his or her shoes. If you were seeking to fill this position, what would you look for in a prospective candidate?

A second type of interviewer you're apt to run into is the individual who talks endlessly about the type of person needed for the job, but who never asks you any questions. If you don't take charge in this situation, you'll leave never having had the opportunity to sell yourself. This type of interviewing style is a clear sign of an inexperienced interviewer. He or she doesn't know what questions to ask, so he or she resorts to talking about a known quantity—the requirements for the job.

You can turn this type of interview to your advantage by listening closely to what the interviewer is saying. Valuable clues are being provided about precisely what the company needs. However, once criteria are mentioned in which you have a particular strength, you need to break in: "I can well understand your need for someone who has designed a computerized accounts payable system. That was an issue I faced when I was with Universal Widgets."

Breaking in requires a great amount of tact. While you want to make sure to get your point across, you don't want to appear as if you are interrupting the interviewer. Try to take advantage of momentary pauses and jump in with your statement. Ironically, if you don't blatantly interrupt the person, he or she will welcome your comments. After all, the interviewer's truly interested in your background, but doesn't know the right questions to ask.

A third type of interviewer you may run into is the person who becomes fixated on one aspect of your résumé. It is often something which has a high curiosity quotient yet does not relate to the requirements for the job. For example, a colleague of mine had played women's professional basketball after graduating from college. Although she also had an impressive business background, recruiters were fascinated with the professional sports experience. It was very difficult for her to get the conversation directed to the business aspects of her background. To avoid having the entire interview revolve around basketball, she would mention that the sports experience had been most valuable to her in teaching skills she used later in business. By relating what she learned in sports to her later career, the conversation quickly moved in the proper direction.

In other cases, these conversations are a result of something that appears in the personal section of your résumé. Individuals with unusual or interesting hobbies, such as billiards, hangliding, or sports handicapping, may wish to remove these activities from their résumé.

Keep in mind that interviewing is not an easy task. A lot rides on the decision whether or not to hire an individual. Unfortunately many companies don't provide adequate training on how to recruit effectively. As a result, it is common for candidates to run into one of the recruiters we've discussed, so it's critical that you be prepared to politely take charge of the interview and ensure that your story is told.

Dealing with Sexual Discrimination

Are you willing to work late nights?

What does your spouse do?

Are you married?

Do you have children?

Do you plan to have children?

Who takes care of your children during the day?

Do any of these questions sound familiar? If so and you're female, you've probably been the victim of sexual discrimination. While many career consultants report that sexual discrimination is less blatant today than in the past (fortunately, questions such as "What type of birth control do you use?" are heard only rarely), the issue is still of real concern to female applicants.

Sexual discrimination is still an issue affecting mostly women, and it most commonly rears its head during an interview. Even in the supposedly enlightened 1990s, female candidates are routinely asked questions not asked of their male counterparts. Although most of these questions are blatantly illegal, they do require some sort of answer. The problem is what type of answer to give. On the one hand you can confront directly the interviewer by stating that you refuse to answer such a question. Although you may be technically correct, you are apt to win the battle and lose the war. In most instances, the only further contact you'll have with the company is a form letter saying, "While we were impressed with your background, we felt that other candidates had stronger and more relevant experience."

So, how do you respond? A question such as, "How do you handle childcare for your kids?" may be illegal, but it is often asked out of practical concern. Even though most employers don't ask this question of their male candidates, child rearing is still predominantly a female responsibility. Employers are concerned that the responsibilities of being a parent will outweigh your responsibilities at work. Although you may find the question intrusive and none of the company's business, an answer that alleviates the interviewer's concern may be the best course of action.

If you do have younger children and are asked this question, a simple statement about the day care service, neighbors, or relatives who help look after your child will suffice. Don't go on and on about the arrangements you've made. That will make you appear defensive. A concise answer, delivered in a confident tone, will usually alleviate employers' concerns.

Some career counselors recommend that if your kids are grown you should initiate the subject on your own. What you don't want is for the male candidate to get the job because the interviewer assumes you have kids at home and wouldn't show up on a regular basis anyway.

Other discriminatory questions that may come up in the interview include the following:

- **What does your husband do?** This question is usually asked to determine job stability. If you say he works for the military or for a Fortune 500 corporation, the assumption may be that you will soon be relocated. Since it takes time for a new employee to learn the ropes, the company wants to be sure you'll be around for a while.

  You may want to bring up that you've made a commitment to a particular city for a specific period of time or that your husband's assignment is for the next five to eight years. If you're applying for a managerial or executive-level job, you might mention that since you're the primary breadwinner, future relocations will be determined by the status of your career.

  Regardless of your earning power compared to your spouse's, it's important to make sure that you don't come across as the "second income." If you do so, you'll invariably be given a lower salary offer. This is a real issue, especially for women working in administrative or secretarial positions. Employers sometimes erroneously assume that a woman's income is discretionary. In most cases, this could not be farther from the truth.

- **Are you willing to work late?** The intent behind this question can range from an innocent inquiry about your willingness to work overtime to a blatant proposition. Your gut feelings toward the interviewer should guide your answer. Remember, if it's the latter, this type of behavior isn't likely to end with the interview. If you're uncomfortable with the direction the conversation is going, it's highly likely that you'll also feel uncomfortable working for that particular company.

The most important point is to determine prior to the interview how you're going to respond to questions like these. Coming across as forthright, regardless of your answer, is far preferable to appearing indecisive or flustered.

CHAPTER 12

FOLLOWING UP

For many people, following up on an interview is an unpleasant though necessary task. Good intentions notwithstanding, employers often do not call back when they say they will. This is highly frustrating to job seekers, who are often unsure what to do. If you call, will you be perceived as aggressive or pushy? Is the company testing you in some way? What is your best course of action?

First, let's examine the steps involved in the follow-up process. Immediately after the interview you should write thank you letters to the managers you met. This can take some time if you spent a full day at the company talking with multiple interviewers. Still, you should invest the time to write each individual a brief note highlighting a particular aspect of your conversation. Although these thank you notes will not get you hired they are often noticed by omission. Many managers consider it simply courtesy to thank people for the time they spent with you.

Although opinions vary, thank you notes can be either handwritten or typed. The legibility of your handwriting will indicate which is more appropriate for you. It is important that the letter arrive very soon after the interview. It is a good idea to write the notes the evening following the meeting when the conversation is still fresh in your mind. Close the letter by reaffirming what you understood the next step to be: "As we discussed, I look forward to hearing your decision within the next two weeks."

What do you do when two weeks pass and there's no word from the prospective employer? Unfortunately, doing nothing, while the easiest course of action, is seldom the correct one. Sometimes employers are testing candidates to determine who is really interested in the opportunity. This is especially true if you are interviewing for a sales position in which tenacity and assertiveness are important components for success. In other cases, the employer simply may not have been able to move the interviewing process along as quickly as he or she had anticipated. In either case, you are better off erring on the side of aggressiveness.

Give the employer a day or two beyond the deadline and then call. Politely use this opportunity to reiterate your interest in the job and attempt to find out when the next step in the interviewing process will take place: "I just wanted to touch base and let you know that I am still very interested in the position we discussed. When do you anticipate making a decision on further interviews?"

Depending on your own comfort in following up on the phone, you may wish to ask questions such as, "At this stage, how does my background compare to that of other candidates you are speaking with?" or "Is there any area of my experience that you have questions or concerns about?" Although some people may feel uncomfortable asking these questions, the answers will give you a clear sense for where you stand as an applicant. One of the most frustrating aspects of the job search process is not knowing how you're doing. Asking these questions will alleviate some of the anxiety.

Don't be overly concerned if your follow-up call is not returned. Employers often have not completed the first round of interviews and no decision has been made. Some hiring managers don't return phone calls just to avoid having to say no decision has been made. Unfortunately, candidates would rather know that fact than languish in the throes of complete uncertainty.

As a general rule of thumb, try not to let more than three weeks go by without some communication with the company. You want to impress the organization with your enthusiasm for the job in addition to remaining a very visible candidate. Some candidates have lost out on opportunities simply because they were forgotten.

You can maintain your presence via both the phone and the mail. For example, if you see an article on the company or the industry send it along to your primary contact with a note saying, "Thought you might be interested in seeing this. I look forward to seeing you again in the near future."

Suffice it to say the follow-up process has to be handled with great sensitivity coupled with an appreciation for what is appropriate given your tenuous relationship with the company. However, many outplacement and career consultants agree that far too many candidates are not aggressive enough. Rather than making you look desperate for a job, following up in the manner described here shows your interest and enthusiasm for the opportunity. These are two critical factors companies look for in candidates.

Part Two

OFFICE ETIQUETTE

CHAPTER 13

STARTING A NEW JOB

Congratulations, next Monday you start your new job! After many long months of frustration and rejection, you've finally accepted a position you're excited about. You're ready to rush in and implement all of the ideas you discussed in the interview. However, when you're starting a new job, it's wise to keep the words of William Shakespeare in mind: "To climb steep hills requires a slow pace at first." While your natural tendency may be to initiate change immediately (after all that's why they hired you, wasn't it?), your best move is to maintain a very low profile.

Many career advisors suggest that you don't try to be a fire-ball on your first day. It's extremely important to take time to observe the culture of the organization. Each company has its own unique style and way of conducting business. You've got to allow yourself sufficient time to learn the subtle nuances about how work gets done within your new organization. Remember that what really counts is long-term results rather than immediate impact.

Political Realities

Don't overlook the fact that there are political issues you will have to address. Take the time to learn the company's politics and how different managers are perceived. You'll want to pick your new business friends carefully. Remember that you're in an environment where you probably don't know anyone. Some of your co-workers may be viewed highly by senior management, whereas others are candidates to go in the first round of layoffs. Who you associate with can have a significant impact on how you're perceived.

As you begin to develop relationships, be careful in whom you confide. Every company has its "Dragon" who exists primarily to pass on gossip about fellow workers. In fact, that individual who latched onto you on day one and now acts like your new best friend is often the Dragon. He or she loves to find out the dirt on people. Since they are often shunned by experienced co-workers, Dragons usually are starving for new friends. Take the time to get the complete lay of the land before you start to develop any significant business relationships.

One of your initial goals should be to try to get to know as many people as quickly as possible. Be proactive in establishing communication with your boss, subordinates, and peers. This type of initiative on your part can ensure that your new job gets off to a positive start.

The Honeymoon

Your first few weeks on the job offer you a unique window of opportunity of which many people unfortunately don't take full advantage. This is sometimes referred to as the "No dumb questions" grace period. Since you are new to the company, now is the time to ask all the simplistic questions you would feel embarrassed or uncomfortable asking six months down the road.

Some people worry that by asking these questions they may make the wrong first impression. Actually, nothing could be further from the truth. Companies give you a honeymoon period to adjust. Although this time varies, most companies expect it to take you between three to six months to settle in completely. After that, you'll be expected to be a fully contributing member of the team. Asking basic questions after the grace period will cause management to wonder about your ability to catch on.

As you settle into your new role, avoid one of the most common temptations for new employees: Never say, "Well at my former company we found it effective to handle that situation this way." Nothing will alienate your new co-workers quicker than constant references to your old company. This will only brand you as an outsider rather than a member of your new organization.

You'll also want to adapt to the look of your new company. When John Sculley went from Pepsi to Apple Computer, one of his first actions was to exchange his corporate pinstripe suits for the more casual attire prevalent in the high-tech community. Observe how your co-workers are dressed and attempt to blend in rather than stand out. Remember, your ability to achieve results will largely depend on how quickly you shed the "outsider" label and become a member of the new team. Seemingly superficial things, such as what you wear to work, can have a great impact on successfully making the transition.

Fitting in, adapting to the language and look of your new company, and getting to know as many people as possible are all important steps in making the right first impression. Be proactive in establishing communication within your new environment to ensure that your new job gets off to a positive start.

CHAPTER 14

SUCCESSFUL DRESSING

It's obvious the applicant just bought the suit. How do you know? Failing to remove the clothing tag on the arm is a dead giveaway. Although you probably won't make a blunder such as this, what you wear to an interview and every day at the office does make a difference.

Interviewers often equate improper business attire with a lack of professionalism. They also know that how you look at the interview is probably the best you're ever going to look. After that, it's all downhill. What should your goal be? Ideally, your appearance should blend into the business environment. You do not want anything you're wearing to distract the interviewer from what you are saying. Err on the side of bland rather than flamboyant.

Guidelines for proper business and interview dress include the following:

- Men should wear suits to interviews unless it is plainly obvious that the position is a "shirt-and-slacks" type of job. In that case, a blue blazer and tie may suffice. However, for the vast majority of professional positions, a business suit is the expected attire. A solid gray or navy blue suit conveys a professional image. Business fashion for women has become less staid. The severe business suits of a few years ago have fortunately fallen out of fashion. Professional businesswomen today have a greater number of options, including jacket-and-skirt combinations, and dresses in conservative colors and patterns.

- Most businesspeople believe that a combination of wool and polyester makes for the ideal combination in a suit. Try for an 80 percent wool, 20 percent polyester mix. Avoid 100% polyester materials; your suit will tend to become shiny. The 80/20 blend of wool and polyester is the best.

- What's the proper length for a man's jacket? A suit coat should be long enough so that, with your arms at your side, your curved fingers can

79

cradle the bottom of the jacket. The coat sleeve should break at your wrist and allow an inch of shirt cuff to show. This is the reason a well-tailored suit jacket will look funny if it's worn with a short-sleeve shirt.

- You may wish to have your tailor add buttons to your suit pants to accommodate suspenders or, as the British call them, "braces." Men should always wear either a belt or suspenders, but never both at the same time. That sends the distinct message that you lack confidence. Your belt should be the same color as your shoes.

   Think of the word "subtlety" when selecting your suspenders. They should reflect the culture of the organization. While wide suspenders with dollar signs or pictures of bulls and bears may be fine on Wall Street, they would hardly be appropriate in many other organizations.

- Men's shirts should be either white or light blue. Button-down collars are the most popular choice among business executives. Although a pure cotton shirt may be the most comfortable, it tends to wrinkle very easily. A blend of polyester and cotton keeps you looking crisp throughout the day. As mentioned before, business professionals do not wear short-sleeve shirts with their suits. Although it can be unbearably hot during the summer, the short-sleeve dress shirt is only appropriate in a few industries and certainly should be avoided in an interview.

- The key point with shoes is that they should be shined, and the heels should not be worn down. Shoes with laces, especially wing tips are the shoe of choice for senior male executives. However, many people find the wing tip hopelessly old-fashioned and opt instead for slip-ons or loafers. These are fine as long as they are conservative and don't have flashy tassels or buckles. For women, a shoe with a modest heel is highly acceptable in virtually any business organization. Overall, it's hard to go wrong with a well-shined pair of black or burgundy shoes in good repair.

- Good choices in ties includes stripes or small patterns. Paisley ties are a lot like liver and onions. When it's cooked just right, it's great. However, the majority of the time it's pretty awful. Ties should be made of silk. Polyester ties are bulkier and consequently more difficult to tie. When tying a tie, the bottom should come just above your belt buckle. The short end should be long enough to fit into the band on the backside of the wider portion.

- Jewelry is a potential trouble area. If you jangle when you walk, you're wearing too much. Women should avoid long, dangling earrings and multiple bracelets. Men should avoid flashy watches and rings. The general rule on jewelry is that men should limit themselves to four pieces, and women should restrict themselves to seven. For example, a man might wear a wedding ring, a watch, and cufflinks. Adding a signet ring to the ensemble would be considered excessive.

If your watch has a built-in alarm that chimes on the hour, do yourself a big favor and turn it off before an interview. Not only will the noise be embarrassing, but it will cause you to lose your concentration.

- Aftershave and perfume should be used sparingly, if at all. No interviewer wants his or her office consumed by the "great smell of Brut." Similarly, women should be modest in their use of makeup.

Many companies have recently begun to allow employees to dress casually on Fridays. What exactly does this mean? In most companies, jeans and shorts are still taboo. Although you don't have to wear a suit and tie, you still want to appear neat and professional. Slacks, a casual shirt or blouse, sweaters, and blazers are all appropriate. One point to keep in mind is that your casual clothes should be freshly laundered and neatly pressed.

Perhaps interviewers place too much emphasis on what you wear to an interview. However, there is a prevailing uniform in corporate America, and candidates are expected to adopt the look. Once you are on board and have established your credibility as a professional, you may have more leeway to individualize your business attire.

Before you go to your next interview or head for work, take a moment to check yourself in the mirror. Is there anything about the way you look that might be considered unprofessional? It is important to both getting and advancing in a job that you always look your best.

CHAPTER 15

INTEROFFICE DATING

Interoffice dating is accompanied by a lot of controversy. An informal random poll showed that a majority of companies formally or informally frown on the practice.

Interoffice dating is a real issue for many people and presents some unique etiquette issues. It's too simplistic to say that you will never date a co-worker. If you eliminate the folks with whom you work, your number of potential dates is drastically reduced. It's difficult to meet members of the opposite sex. There aren't a lot of places you can go to meet new people, and many people don't like to hang around bars. More of us are living in areas of the country far removed from where we grew up. Thus, the traditional matchmaking role played by immediate family members is significantly reduced.

Opinions vary, but the general consensus is that if you're attracted to a co-worker there's nothing improper about asking him or her out. Lunch, Sunday brunch, or sporting events are low-pressure outings that can help the two of you make the transition from a professional to a personal relationship. Of course, there are some people at work you shouldn't date:

- Your boss

- Your subordinates

- Someone who's married

- Customers or clients

It's perfectly acceptable for a man to ask a woman out or vice versa. More women feel comfortable asking a man out if the get-together is relatively casual in nature.

If the two of you become a couple, remember the etiquette that such a relationship demands. First, be discreet. This doesn't mean you have to keep it a secret, since you probably couldn't even if you tried. The tom-toms of the corporate grapevine seem to pick up rumors faster than any other mechanism known to man or woman. However, once your relationship becomes public knowledge, the interaction you have with your other co-workers is bound to change. How much it changes and whether that change is positive or negative will largely depend on you.

What are the possible reactions? They range considerably. Some people may start to think of you in the context of your new relationship, rather than as a professional in the workforce. This is a particularly sensitive issue if your boss learns about the relationship. You will have to take proactive steps to address these issues if you want to nip them in the proverbial bud.

A fact of life is that, if you engage in a relationship with a co-worker, you need to be prepared to be the topic, at least in the short-term, of office gossip. There will be speculation about how the two of you met, what your relationship is like, and other areas you can readily imagine. Some of your office mates may start to distant themselves from you. This is especially likely if they have a business relationship with your partner. "Pillow talk" is of real concern to your co-workers. Additionally, in the fledgling stages of the relationship, no one, yourselves included, knows exactly how long it will last. A volcanic end may obliterate innocent bystanders. Thus, don't be surprised if you experience a certain amount of wariness from those with whom you've historically enjoyed a warm and candid relationship.

While each relationship is unique, there is one cardinal rule of interoffice dating you would be wise to follow. First and foremost, please eliminate any hugging, kissing, soulful glances, or other outward displays of affection while in the office or at other company-sponsored events.

Even though your relationship with your co-workers initially may be somewhat tense or uncomfortable, this will change over time. If your relationship takes hold, you will become less of a novelty and more a part of the tapestry of company life. Gossip feeds off change, not constancy. Sooner or later (hopefully sooner), some other event will supersede you as the topic for the day. However, should the two of you break up, you can expect to once again be thrust into the limelight of the company gossip mill.

Even when your relationship is no longer the topic of the month, this does not necessarily mean that your business relationships within the company will automatically revert back to the way they were before the relationship. Accomplishing this may require some initiative on your part. Remember, you can't be a wimp in this world and expect to reap a whole lot of benefits. While it's certainly easier to refuse to acknowledge that relationships have changed, this won't help rebuild bridges that are important for your career success. The trick is to confront the issues once you become aware of them. The office grapevine will alert you to the facts. Despite all that is said about gossip, the sad fact is that most of it is at least partially true. We tend to blindly believe what we hear regardless of whether it makes sense. Once rumors spread about your relationship, individuals will react to it based on their own relationships with you and how it potentially affects their careers.

The most important person with whom you need to discuss this is your boss. It's also a very difficult conversation to have, and your comfort level in raising the topic will depend on your relationship with him or her. It may be helpful to raise the subject under the general auspices of seeking advice. You might try something like, "Boss, you may have heard that I've begun a relationship with Terry. Quite frankly, we entered into the relationship with some concerns about how others in the company might view it. We've made the commitment that we don't discuss business issues affecting our respective departments between us, yet I'm a little concerned about how others might be viewing our dating. Is there any advice you can offer?"

This puts your cards on the table in a straightforward and humble manner. Most bosses will respond positively to this initiative and may in fact give you some practical advice on how to navigate the potentially rocky shoals. You can raise the subject in a similar manner with co-workers and other peers within your organization. By taking the well-known bull by the horns, you are likely to find that others' negative preconceptions about your relationship fade and the old working relationships quickly reassert themselves.

CHAPTER 16

BEING A GOOD INTERVIEWER

In Part One, we discussed some principles of being a good interviewee. Now let's put the shoe on the other foot. By thinking about the etiquette rules for being a good interviewer you can not only increase your ability to select the right people for your departments, but also gain a new appreciation for the challenges that go into the hiring process. No matter how uncomfortable we may feel at being interviewed, few of us have stopped to think about what it's like on the other side of the desk. Managers who have been in both roles often comment that being the interviewer is equally as difficult as being the candidate.

It's not surprising that interviewing is such a difficult task. The outcome of an interview has far-reaching consequences. Most of the decisions a supervisor makes during the day can be corrected with little adverse effect if they are discovered to be incorrect. This is not the case with a hiring decision. If I decide to hire you and you perform well, this reflects favorably on me. In many companies, the ability to spot and develop talent is a requirement for advancement to upper middle management positions. However, if I hire you and you don't work out, I will bear a good part of the criticism for recruiting you in the first place. Thus, interviewing is a risky management task.

Another factor that makes interviewing difficult is an uncertainty as to what questions you should ask. Interviewers sometimes think there is one magical question that will determine if a candidate is suitable for the position. Of course, the magical question doesn't exist and this sometimes leads interviewers to ask questions that are either inappropriate or simply bizarre. I once worked with a senior-level manager who insisted on asking candidates, "If this company were a car, what type of car would it be?" When asked why he posed this question and what possible useful information could be learned from the answer, the manager simply stated that he liked the question. This is a common problem supervisors face in an interview. They ask questions because they read them in a book, remember being asked the same questions once in an interview, or simply like the sound of a particular question. An important first step for successful interviewing is to make sure your questions are relevant to the position you have open. How will the candidate's answer assist you in making an employment decision?

Successful interviewers are prepared. Far too many supervisors only glance at a candidate's résumé prior to the interview. This results in valuable time being wasted having the applicant simply reciting what could have been learned by studying the résumé before hand. For example, a candidate may have participated in a project similar to one you are now initiating. It is important for you to get specific, detailed information about the role he or she played. Always follow up when the words "performed on a team" appear on a résumé. You want to determine the exact nature of the involvement. The candidate may have held a leadership role or been the team member who brought in the coffee. In either case, you want to know. Far too many interviewers get burned by making assumptions without following up. Candidates often tend to talk in generalities, so it is important to encourage them to speak about specific roles they 've played. Questions such as "How exactly did you accomplish that task?" or "What was your specific area of responsibility?" help get at this important information. Some interviewers find it helpful to actually write questions down on the résumé so they don't forget them during the conversation.

An effective method of starting off an interview is to ask the candidate why he or she applied for the position. The answer will provide you with some valuable information. If the candidate's response is vague, you can assume he or she did little homework and probably is just trying to go on as many interviews as possible. If, however, he or she responds with enthusiasm that he or she believes there is a good match between his or her background and the requirements of the position, this is a good early sign. Make sure to follow up and ask applicants what specific skills they feel they have that would be of benefit to the assignment.

Make sure your environment is conducive to interviewing. If you work in a cubicle, try to reserve a conference room or some other quiet area in which to conduct the interview. Forward your phone and concentrate on the individual sitting in front of you. Don't be overly impressed with a person who dresses perfectly and looks the part. He or she may have little substance beyond a nice suit.

A basic principle of successful interviewing is that the past is a strong predictor of the future. People who have been successful in the past are likely to replicate that behavior again. Thus, make sure you focus your interview energies on identifying specific situations in which the applicant performed a specific task. Collecting this type of information will make you more comfortable with your ultimate decision on whether to hire that individual.

CHAPTER 17

WORKING WITH A
DIFFICULT BOSS

The appeal of such movies as *9 to 5* and *Working Girl* are considerable. The obnoxious boss gets well-deserved punishment, and faithful workers triumph over adversity. Ah, if only the real world were so simple.

How American business selects its managers is an imprecise art. In most cases, your boss became a supervisor because he or she was good at a particular task. For example, consider the person whose job is to repair computers. If this individual performs well he or she stands a good chance of being promoted to a supervisory position. In the new assignment, instead of actually doing computer repair work, the newly minted manager has to motivate other people to repair the computers. This demands a completely different set of skills from the technical ability of fixing the machines.

Successful supervision is largely learned through trial and error. Truly effective managers have a repertoire of supervisory skills at their disposal. Successful managers typically have had a range of experience, including motivating teams and working with problem individuals. They have come to understand that each person needs something slightly different from his or her manager.

Identifying leaders who have the ability to motivate others is a continuing challenge for American businesses. Companies often look for what they call an individual's "Tom Sawyer" potential. To what extent can you get other people to paint your white picket fence for you? Since developing management skills requires exposure to a variety of business situations, a lack of perspective accounts for most of the problems rookie managers face.

What this means is that in your career you are very likely to work for a number of managers who have not yet developed the skills necessary to be truly effective as supervisors. Some individuals ultimately have little interest in developing these skills, while others are only limited by their experience of how to deal with certain situations.

Unfortunately, difficult bosses are a reality that most of us have to deal with at some point in our careers. Such bosses display a range of behaviors, tending to be temperamental, secretive, indecisive, and/or unpredictable. Your ability to deal with a difficult boss depends in large part on your level of self-esteem. Individuals with low self-esteem allow themselves to overreact and become potential casualties. These people often find themselves in job after job as a result of personalizing the criticism they receive from their bosses.

Although quitting your job does offer an escape from a difficult boss, it isn't a viable option for most of us. Regardless of our circumstances and experiences, let's be frank, good jobs are hard to come by. The good news is that most exasperating bosses aren't that way all the time. In fact, most of them are actually good businesspeople, although their people skills may leave something to be desired. The trick is to avoid reacting personally to your boss's behavior.

To deal effectively with a difficult boss, you've got to put your feelings toward him or her on hold so you can focus on the content of what he or she says. Remember that no matter how difficult your boss may be, he or she is a person with fears, foibles, and aspirations. Keep in mind that we all tend to act a little out of character when we're under great amounts of stress and strain. If your boss is a person who reacts this way to pressure, you're likely to receive the brunt of the Hyde side of what might otherwise be a Dr. Jekyll personality.

The problem with these types of individuals is that they can make you feel like you're back in a parent-child relationship. When you feel like a child in your job, it is virtually impossible to maintain the emotional distance that is critical for handling a difficult boss. Emotional distancing is very important in minimizing your reactions and maintaining control. Psychologist Peter Wylie, author of *Problem Bosses: Who They Are and How to Deal with Them*, says, "If you choose to deal with fear by scurrying away from it, the problem is going to continue to recur. You're going to be treated in less than an adult way. If you confront it in a respectful way, you're much likelier to get the relationship off the destructive parent-child plane."

So what steps can you take to deal with a difficult boss? Here are some ideas:

- State your feelings to your boss in a constructive and professional manner. Resist the temptation to blow up, whine, or complain. For example, say, "When you yell at me in front of the others, I get embarrassed and upset. I'm not able to give you my best effort when I feel as if I'm being personally attacked." This type of statement lets the boss know how his or her comments are perceived, which is often quite different than what he or she intended.

- Gauge the intent behind the words. Although the message may be communicated in a manner you don't like, take time to decide if the content of the message is accurate. Most of us don't like criticism, regardless of how sugarcoated it is. Reflect on your boss's criticisms and try to benefit from them. Have you really given your best effort, or are you hurting your boss's credibility by not putting forth 100 percent? Your boss may seem to be paranoid, but he or she also may be right.

- A common challenge is the boss who likes to micromanage. Such managers want to know what you're doing at what often seem like five-minute intervals. If they don't like what they hear or your work isn't up to their standards, they aren't reluctant to redo your work. The concept of delegation has never really sunk in with these managers. What to do?

  First, recognize that you are not going to be able to change your supervisor's behavior overnight. Most micromanagers are driven by insecurity. They are terribly concerned that you are going to make them look bad and, consequently, are constantly looking over your shoulder. The following tactic tends to work well with this type of manager. Since they are insecure, you've got to work on building credibility, which takes time. Micromanagers love detail, so be prepared for meetings and anticipate any follow-up questions your boss might ask. As you gain your supervisor's confidence, you will find that nitpicking questions will begin to diminish. Remember that this trust has to be earned over time; don't become impatient when it isn't immediately forthcoming.

- A key rule for developing a positive relationship with any boss is to keep him or her informed. No manager likes to be surprised. An effective method to make sure you are keeping your boss up to speed is to schedule regular meetings with him or her. Although this would seem obvious, it's surprising how much management communication is conducted informally. You can't afford to rely on chance meetings as the sole means of keeping your boss informed on what's going on in your area.

- A common error subordinates make is failing to offer solutions when problems are identified. It's simply not enough to dump your problems in your manager's lap. Think through what your options are and develop a number of alternative solutions. Managers won't penalize you if they don't agree with your recommendations. However, you'll lose points if you don't offer any suggestions.

A week may seem like an eternity when you are stuck with a bad boss. Don't let a poor supervisor cause you to leave what is otherwise a great job. Remember, you'll probably work for many different bosses over the lifetime of your career. Turnover in supervisors is quite high so, when faced with a bad boss, exercise a little patience. Chances are you may be able to outlast him or her.

There's no one clear-cut, simplistic solution to dealing with a difficult boss. You may need to take comfort in the knowledge that "what goes around, comes around." Most truly difficult bosses eventually get hoisted on their own petards. Says Carole Hyatt, coauther of *When Smart People Fail,* "The major reason smart people fail is because they lack interpersonal skills. Bosses who support and help people know those people will help them. It's just smart strategy. If you make a lot of enemies, you're going to ultimately fail."

CHAPTER 18

HANDLING STRESS

When you talk with human resources managers and career counselors, a common subject is stress in the workplace. Even if you managed to avoid the most recent round of layoffs, you'll probably find yourself under more pressure at work. "Lean and mean" may be a popular catchphrase for the '90s, but it translates into an increasing number of individuals suffering from job burnout.

What are the signs of burnout? The most common indication is a feeling of working harder and harder without accomplishing anything. Similar to running on a treadmill, you go faster and faster, yet you never actually get anywhere. Many individuals experiencing burnout have enormous difficulty in determining how their work contributes to the goals of their organization.

When you view new assignments as burdens instead of opportunities, it's time to take specific steps to readjust your thinking. Left untreated, burnout can cause severe problems for both you and your employer. It's hard to hide your emotions from your co-workers and boss. If you dread new assignments, the quality of your work is likely to be unsatisfactory. The good news is you'll become the last person to be given a new assignment; the bad news is your reputation as a team player and contributor will evaporate because you can no longer be counted on to pull your weight in the office. The next time there's a layoff, guess whose name will be at the top of the list?

There are a couple of methods you can use to readjust your attitude and turn the situation around. Since one of the most common symptoms of burnout is feeling that your work just doesn't matter, tackling this issue head-on is a good first step. Take time to analyze what you do at work. Think about and write down everything you do from the moment you arrive till you leave at the end of the day. After you've completed this step, write down why you think you're asked to perform each task and who in the company benefits from your efforts. Although you may find this difficult initially, you'll discover that this exercise stimulates your creative juices and often quickly dispel that feeling of "Why am I even bothering to do this work, since no one cares?"

A second solution to burnout can take more time but is also effective. Visualize your ideal job. Think about the elements of your work that you truly enjoy and that stimulate you. Is it the opportunity to be creative, help others, or work by yourself? Sometimes completing a psychological assessment instrument, such as the Campbell Inventory, can help you identify these elements. Armed with this information, think about your current job. Is there a way to modify or change your present job to allow you to experience more of the things you enjoy? This often requires that you have a candid discussion with your supervisor, but the result can be extremely positive.

For example, Wanda was a word processing operator experiencing burnout. She saw her job as one endless routine, and she lacked a clear sense of purpose. Over a three-month period, her work went from highly satisfactory to unacceptable, and she was in imminent danger of being fired. Fortunately, Wanda sought counseling and took the time to visualize her ideal job. Based on this assessment, she concluded that she most enjoyed jobs in which she could be creative, advise others, and participate in the communication process. In a subsequent conversation with her boss, Wanda suggested that the firm buy a graphics software package for the computer system. Wanda knew the company had long talked about improving the quality of its newsletter, and she made a deal with her employer. If the company would purchase the software package, Wanda would learn the system in her spare time. Today, Wanda is highly stimulated in her job, the newsletter looks great, and her company has identified many other applications for Wanda's new skill in graphic design.

Obviously, this improvement didn't occur overnight. It took time for Wanda to identify how she could make her job more interesting. Her eventual success was also dependent on the relationship she had with her supervisor. Most supervisors are very receptive to employees like Wanda who have always been productive but hit a snag in the momentum department. The important point is that burnout doesn't have to result in quitting or being fired from your job. If you're suffering from burnout, take the necessary steps to reinvigorate yourself and your work.

CHAPTER 19

LEAVING ON THE RIGHT NOTE

Finally, all of your work pays off. An exciting job at a competitive salary has been offered and you've accepted. You're ready to begin a new chapter in your career. However, before you start your new job, it's important to leave your current employer in the most professional way possible.

Giving notice requires sensitivity and tact. Remember that your leaving will cause problems for your supervisor. Someone will have to pick up the slack created by your absence. This is likely to be a real concern to your former boss, especially since much of the burden is likely to fall on his or her shoulders.

Don't Burn Any Bridges

When giving notice it is important not to burn any bridges. It's impossible to predict who you may wind up working with in the future. A former supervisor might resurface at your new company. This is especially true for individuals in certain professions, such as advertising or investments, where turnover is common and the likelihood of colleagues working together in a new employment situation is high. Thus, it is important that your departure be handled as gracefully as possible.

You might be tempted to copy customer files or take other confidential information with you when you leave. Although you may believe these documents will help you get your new job off to a quick start, use your common sense and forgo the temptation: This tactic usually backfires. Employers invariably discover what you've taken and, in certain cases, may pursue legal recourse. It's also doubtful that your new boss will be pleased with this type of initiative. He or she will probably conclude that your overall business ethics are less than honorable.

Andrea Hershatter, Assistant Dean of Emory University's Business School, points out that it's a good idea to review any noncompete agreements you may have signed prior to giving notice. This is especially prudent if it's been a number of years since you last reviewed these documents. You may find that an agreement specifically precludes you from going to work for a local competitor or places other restrictions on what you can do in your new job. These agreements can often be renegotiated before you leave. You'll want to discuss the restrictions you're facing candidly with your new boss before giving notice. However, don't assume that noncompete agreements aren't enforceable—they are.

Former co-workers may contact you to inquire about opportunities with your new employer. Be careful here and don't cross the ethical line. Give former co-workers the name of a person to whom they can send their résumé is fine; actively recruiting co-workers isn't.

Communicating the News

It's always a good idea to have your new offer in writing before actually giving notice to your current employer. Once you have that piece of paper in hand, schedule a meeting with your boss to break the news. Whatever you do, don't send a memo or just grab your boss in the hallway. The former is far too impersonal, and the latter is unprofessional. Schedule a meeting but defer from mentioning the subject. Deflect your boss's curiosity by saying that the subject is something you would rather discuss face to face.

In the meeting, be straightforward. Don't hedge or waffle about the purpose of the discussion. Explain your new opportunity in the context of a situation that was too good to pass up. Despite your personal opinions of your old job or boss, now is not the time to vent them. All of us have fantasized about resigning and telling the boss off once and for all. Although this may have great appeal, it is an act you may later regret.

Keep the tone of your conversation positive. Mention how you have enjoyed the opportunity to work for your current employer and how much you have learned from your supervisor. Even though you and your boss may not have agreed on a lot of issues, there is usually something that you learned from the experience. You might say something such as, "I know we didn't always see eye to eye on some of the methods used to increase sales, but I must admit you forced me to consider alternatives that I probably would have dismissed without trying if you hadn't insisted."

How Much Notice?

The discussion will inevitably move to how long you will keep working. At this point, your goals and those of your boss are likely to differ. You probably will want to leave your old employer as quickly as possible, whereas your supervisor usually will want you to stick around to ensure an orderly transition. Many supervisors would like you to stay until a replacement can be found. However, since this might take months, a compromise has to be struck.

Standard separation practice calls for you to give two weeks notice. Try to be flexible if you were in the middle of a project and a little extra time is needed to complete a crucial segment of work. You can score points with your former boss by volunteering to recommend other individuals to take your place. Develop a list of potential internal and external candidates. This type of gesture carries a lot of weight and positions you as someone who wants to make the transition go as smoothly as possible.

Career consultant Harvey Brickley believes the standard two weeks notice is still adequate. Unless there is an important project to be wrapped up, you shouldn't feel obligated to stay longer. However, don't be surprised if your offer to stay two weeks is declined and you're asked to leave permanently at the end of the day. Many employers believe that once you've made the decision to quit, there's little advantage, aside from an orderly transition, in having you hang around. Thus, is you're asked to wrap up your business, clean out your desk, and leave, don't take it personally.

The Pitfalls of Counteroffers

You may receive a counteroffer from your former employer, which is usually not a good idea to accept. Once you give notice, your loyalty to the company will always be in question. Counteroffers are often used to buy employers time to find a permanent replacement for you. Thus, accepting a counteroffer usually comes back to haunt you down the road.

Receiving a counteroffer is flattering and seductive. You are showered with reasons why you should not leave good old XYZ Corp. The praise and perhaps additional money are powerful inducements for you to stay. However, when all the dust settles, it is usually a terrible mistake to accept a counteroffer.

Let's define our terms. *Counteroffers* are those inducements your current employer uses to get you to stay once you have announced your intentions of accepting a new position. Although there may be a few individuals who have accepted such an offer and gone on to have a successful career with their current employers, their numbers are few. For most people, the counteroffer does nothing to address the underlying issues behind their decision to seek new employment. Management recruiters and human resources executives estimate that up to 80 percent of workers who accept counteroffers subsequently leave their employers within one year.

The main reason counteroffers don't work is the somewhat antiquated notion of loyalty. Although we can argue in this age of downsizings and restructurings that employee loyalty is a thing of the past, a strong sense of loyalty still exists between supervisors and their employees. Accepting an offer from another company upsets that bond. It's not your loyalty to good old XYZ Corp. that is being called into question, but your loyalty to your department. Thus, a boss's reaction is commonly a very personal and negative one: "How could you do this to me?"

On the pragmatic level, when you announce your planned departure, business plans are upset, work must be redistributed, vacations are postponed, and life generally becomes much more difficult for everyone in the department. Given this upheaval, it's not surprising counteroffers are made. Supervisors may say, "Let's keep Nancy here at least until the first quarter is over so we can complete the Fornortnor financing." Keeping you around so current projects can be completed is a compelling reason to offer you attractive inducements to stay. However, remember what the motivation behind the offer is. Suddenly you've moved from a long-term player to a short-term issue that needs to be handled. Guess who won't be getting a whole lot of new critical assignments in the future? Guess who becomes extremely expendable once the Fornortnor financing is completed? It's likely you'll only enjoy the benefits of the counteroffer for a few months while the company immediately begins to scout around for your replacement.

Career change advisors and recruiters urge you to consider the following universal truths before succumbing to the temptations of a counteroffer:

1. If the only way you can get a raise or promotion is to threaten to quit, you're probably better off somewhere else.

2. No matter what your supervisor says when making the counteroffer, your loyalty will always be suspect. You will not longer be viewed as a team player, and you may find yourself dropped from the inner circle of decision makers.

3. Counteroffers are usually little more than stalling devices to give your company time to find your replacement.

4. The original frustrations you had with your employer are not likely to change. Your reasons for leaving will still exist. All the counteroffer does is improve some of the superficial circumstances or provide a short-term financial compensation.

So, if you've decided to accept a new position and receive a counteroffer, remember the motivation behind the offer. The odds are against you if you accept. Take the counteroffer as a compliment but don't let it obscure the more fundamental reasons you decided to conduct a job search in the first place.

Tying Up Loose Ends

Once you have accepted a new job, inform all of the contacts you made by networking about your good news. Draft a letter that thanks them for their assistance and discusses the scope of your new position. Include your new company address and phone number. Send this letter to everyone with whom you came in contact with during your job search, regardless of whether they actually helped you. After all, you never know when you might need them again.

People tend to remember you by the last impression you make. If your exit from an organization is confrontational and bitter, your words may come back to haunt you. Conversely, if you don't ruffle any management feathers, you'll be remembered in a favorable light and perhaps realize some career benefits down the road. Ultimately, most of us want to be remembered positively. By avoiding some of the more common mistakes, you can ensure that your transition to your new job proceeds with the blessing of your former employer.

Part Three

SOCIAL AND TRAVEL ETIQUETTE

CHAPTER 20

CONVERSATION BASICS

An important component of career success in all its forms, from finding the right job to negotiating an important contract, is communication. Communicating well is critical for breaking in and succeeding. People who have mastered the art of being good conversationalists impress all of us, yet it's an area in which a lot of us are lacking. Is it a natural skill, or one that can be learned? The answer is yes to both questions.

Of course, certain people have a natural proclivity for verbal communication. These are the folks who from an early age are quick with a retort and never seem at a loss for words. Certainly, these individuals have an easier time of developing the necessary skills for verbal repartee. However, just because you don't have a natural "gift of gab" doesn't mean you can't become a scintillating conversationalist.

The first step to becoming an effective conversationalist is to conduct a voice audit. The best way to conduct this audit is to listen to yourself on tape. You don't need to prepare a speech and deliver it in front of a microphone. Rather, purchase a small tape recorder (you shouldn't have to spend more than $50) and record yourself the next time you're on the phone or speaking with someone in your office. (You should always inform the other person that they are being recorded.)

Listening to yourself on tape is an eye-opening experience for most people. The most common reaction is, "Gee, I didn't know I sounded like that!" How we hear ourselves in our heads is quite different than how others hear us. Expect to be somewhat surprised the first time you listen to yourself. However, if you repeat this exercise on a regular basis, you'll eventually become familiar with the sound of your voice.

The one advantage to having your voice sound unfamiliar is that it makes it easy for you to provide a critical review of the voice you're hearing on the tape. As you listen to yourself, get out a pad of paper and assess your voice on the following components:

- **Enunciation.** Are you easy to understand, or do your words run together in a blur of sound?

- **Breathing.** Are you able to articulate a relatively long statement without having annoying breaths occur halfway through the sentence? Frequent, ill-timed breathing gives the impression of a person who may be indecisive or someone who lacks self-confidence. This problem is particularly noticeable if you conduct much business on the telephone.

- **Pitch and tone.** If the pitch of your voice is too high, you'll tend to sound nervous. If your voice is harsh, you may be perceived as brusque or having poor people skills.

- **Pace.** Variation is the key. While you don't want to speak too fast or too slowly, never changing the pace at which you speak can quickly put your listener to sleep.

- **Emotion.** Does your voice convey enthusiasm and interest in the other person? A flat, unresponsive tone may give the impression that you are uncaring or uninterested.

- **Accent.** Is your voice largely devoid of a pronounced regional accent? While a thick New York accent won't raise eyebrows in New York City, it can potentially damage your credibility if you're trying to do business in Nashville. Conversely, a pronounced Southern accent conjures up an image of a hayseed in many areas of the country. (Of course many Southerners have intentionally increased their accents during important negotiations to create this illusion.) Overall, it's best if your voice merely hints, rather than shouts, that you hail from a particular area of the country.

- **Words.** The words you use also play a major role in how you are perceived. Although a good vocabulary is an important tool for the adept conversationalist, using hundred-dollar words for their own sake gives others the exact opposite impression of your capabilities.

If, based on analyzing your voice on tape, you think one of these areas is a problem, there are various resources you can take advantage of to eliminate or reduce the problem. As a first step, you might call your local college or university and ask to be connected with the communications department. Very often the instructors and professors accept individuals as clients to supplement their teaching work. If you don't mind working on your problem in a group setting, continuing education programs offered by many four-year and community colleges offer a very cost-effective solution. Most larger communities have private consultants who can offer you more individ-ualized attention. They can be found most easily in the Yellow Pages under "Communications," "Voice Training," or "Speech." You also might check with recording studios in your area for referrals.

While possessing an attractive voice is an important component in be-coming an accomplished conversationalist, it's only one aspect. Other key components include body language and the ability to listen. In fact, many accomplished managers believe the key to being a highly effective conversa-tionalist has more to do with listening than speaking. The subjects of body language and listening are critical aspects in conversation etiquette and are covered in greater detail in Chapters 21 and 22.

One thing that separates good conversationalists from those who struggle is their attitude. Good conversationalists always seem interested in what you're saying. Whether they really are isn't the point. What is important is that they always act as if you are the most important person in the world to them at that particular point in time. The ability to hide your boredom and appear interested in what another person is saying is a time-honored skill that we would all be well advised to develop.

How do you inadvertently signal boredom? The most common way is to continually look over the shoulder of the person with whom you're talking. We've probably all been guilty of this at some point in time. We've all also been recipients of this behavior. Remember how you felt? The unde-niable impression was that the person was interested in talking with anyone but you. This message is the exact opposite of what a good conversational-ist's goal.

The key to not showing you're bored largely goes back to attitude. Become a firm believer that we can learn something from most anyone. If you enter into a conversation thinking it will be boring, you'll rarely be disappointed. Conversely, if you enter into a conversation with the goal of learning something new, you'll also rarely be disappointed. If you mentally decide that you will be interested in what a person is saying, you'll find that you actually do become interested.

In addition to having a real interest in other people, good conversational-ists tend to share some other common traits and characteristics. Good con-versationalists are avid readers of a variety of magazines, newspapers, and books. As billionaire record mogul David Geffen commented in the October 1994 edition of *Vanity Fair* on the New Establishment: "It's important to read about what's happening, to meet people who are doing things, to know what people are reading, what they're seeing. I can't wait for my newspapers to be delivered. I can't wait for my new magazines to come."

This doesn't mean you have to become an expert on every known subject. However, it's important that you become somewhat knowledge-able about a wide range of subjects. You want to develop a broad enough range so that you can quickly switch subjects from business to the arts to politics. Although many serious journalists disdain a newspaper such as *USA Today,* it serves as a valuable tool for the conversationalist. Each edition, in a relatively short period of time, allows you to "get up to speed" on what's been going on in the world of arts, business, sports, and current events. Additionally, having this broad base of information at the tip of your tongue allows you to tailor your conversation to the person with whom you've speaking.

Along with being knowledgeable about current events, it's also a good idea to have some questions in mind. Asking the right question at the right time is one of the hallmarks of good conversation etiquette. In fact, many adept conversationalists believe that asking questions is the most important aspect of carrying on a good conversation. Says one such executive, "I tend to find that the most interesting conversations I have are those in which I do very little talking." Remember, you learn more when your listening then when you're talking. It may be somewhat ironic but, by asking stimulating questions, you'll quickly become known as a brilliant conversationalist.

While it's easy for most of us to answer questions, coming up with the right questions takes some preparation. As with any other business etiquette skill, the more you practice, the more adept and comfortable you'll become with this process. Good questions stimulate and sustain conversation. You will want to vary the type of questions you ask depending on the nature of the occasion. Some fundamental questions for a business gathering, association meeting, or similar function might include:

- What type of business are you in?

- How is your business doing? (Always a good question unless *The Wall Street Journal* has just run a front-page story on the imminent demise of the person's company—another good reason to keep up with your current events.)

- How long have you been a member of this association? Have you found it worthwhile?

- What's your role at XYZ Company?

Current events questions with an emphasis on local/national news and business, the arts, and sports are better for a social get-together:

- How do you know our host/hostess?

- Have you lived in this area long?

- Any recommendations on where to go for (some service you're considering purchasing)?

In any situation, a standard fallback, if you've completely drawn a blank, is to compliment the surroundings, decor, food, or (as an absolutely last resort) the weather.

Avoiding Conversational Gaffes and Faux Pas

As in any area of etiquette, it's important to know both what you should be doing and what to avoid. The following rules apply to any business or social conversation.

- **Don't interrupt.** This is a common problem for many of us. The reason so many of us interrupt each other is that we hear a lot faster than we talk. As a result, we tend to fall into the habit of finishing sentences for other people. This is especially an issue when Northerners (who tend to speak quickly) have conversations with people from the South (who tend to speak s-l-o-w-l-y). Check your impatience and hold your tongue until the speaker is finished.

- **Don't correct pronunciation or grammar.** We all have pet peeves concerning words that others butcher. Unfortunately, our good intentions to educate others about their mistakes usually isn't well received. For example, my pet peeve regards the term "irregardless." Although it's used extensively by lots of people, it's unfortunately not a word. The correct word is "regardless," about which I have been known to educate one and all. It's a struggle for me to bite my tongue when someone says "irregardless," but I've found the reaction to my attempts to educate to be the greater of two evils.

- **Don't focus on just one person.** When you're in a group conversation, ask questions of everyone in the group and establsih eye contact with all of the participants. At a dinner party, make sure you engage in conversation with the person both to your right and your left.

- **Don't bore other people.** Be sensitive to the fact that you may not be as charming and witty as you think you are. Pay attention to the body language of others. When they start shifting their weight or that glazed look comes across their eyes, it's time to shift the conversation.

- **Don't talk about money.** Sure, we're all curious about how much others make, how much their house cost, or the amount of alimony they're paying, but, as we all know, it's rude to actually ask.

- **Don't encourage gossip.** Again, it's a tempting subject but one from which no one benefits. The only person who impresses others is the one who says, "Well, it's all speculation at this point in time, so it's hard to know what's going on." Comments such as these tend to make the rest of the group realize that spreading rumors serves no honorable goal.

- **Avoid the obvious.** The general rule is that whatever is on this week's cover of *The National Enquirer* is not a topic for mature adults to discuss. Unless the celebrity is personally known to you (or you were also abducted by aliens) avoid these subjects like the plague. They mark you as an unsophisticated lightweight with a limited range of interests.

- **Your children.** Aside from a brief conversation about if you have them, their sex, and how old they are, no one outside of your immediate family is really all that interested. Use the topic only as an ice-breaker, or if you completely run out of things to ask.

Keep these points in mind and you'll find both your comfort with and skill at conversation will increase.

CHAPTER 21

THE IMPORTANCE OF LISTENING

If you're going to be a successful job candidate or businessperson, you've got to be a good listener. Unfortunately, many of us suffer from poor listening skills. Since we tend to be nervous in interviews or meetings, we are apt to interrupt, become distracted, or assume we know what the question is before it is complete. All of these can spell doom to the success of an encounter.

For instance, we often are faced with someone who speaks very s-l-o-w-l-y. It seems like forever before the words finally come out of his or her mouth. In these situations, our tendency is to complete the sentence for the speaker. While this can expedite the process, it makes a negative impression. You must learn to bite your tongue and wait for the speaker to conclude what he or she is saying no matter how long it takes. This is a common problem since we can hear and comprehend much faster than we can speak. Thus, even with individuals who speak at a normal rate of speed, you may find yourself tempted to finish their sentences. Resist the temptation. Establishing a relationship between yourself and another person is critical to conducting business successfully. Interrupting the speaker only distracts from the development of this relationship.

In an interview situation, experienced interviewees often face a different issue. About halfway through the speaker's question, you think you know what is going to be asked. You stop listening and begin formulating in your mind how you are going to respond. Unfortunately, what often occurs is that the question actually asked is different than the one you anticipated. Consequently, you give an answer which misses the mark. If you ever notice that the interviewer is looking at you with a somewhat quizzical look on his or her face, you can assume you are answering the wrong question. The result is the interviewer thinking, "Interesting answer, I wonder why you're telling me this." Remember, you'll be nervous in an interview. When you're nervous, you often have a tendency to anticipate events before they actually occur. Make sure you fully hear each question before you begin to formulate a response.

Distractions are another issue that can affect your ability to listen effectively. Murphy's Law prophesies that window washers will begin their work precisely at the moment you are meeting. You may also discover that there are all sorts of interesting things on the office walls and desk. I once went to a meeting in which the manager kept playing with a toy ray gun (at least, I though it was a toy). Suffice it to say, you can become distracted quickly if you become fascinated with the stuff in the office, rather then the words coming out of the other person's mouth.

The telephone offers it own unique listening challenges. You spend a lot of time on the phone in almost any job or job search. Since you're not face to face with the speaker, it's especially important that you make sure you're correctly hearing what he or she is saying. A lot of the "clues" that you would otherwise easily pick up, can be overlooked if you're not careful. Whit Blakeley, partner of the outplacement firm Career Management International, points out how important it is to really listen to what the person on the other end of the line is saying: "Suppose you're following up on a 'hot' lead, and you know the company quickly wants to hire someone. If the contact's secretary indicates that the person will be away from the office for an extended period of time, your immediate reaction may be to call the person back once he or she has returned. However, if you listen to this clue, you would surmise that someone else is probably temporarily taking over your contact's responsibilities and ask for that name."

Listening is especially important when you encounter someone who asks you a series of rapid-fire questions back to back. In this situation, it's important not be become flustered and attempt to answer all of the questions at once. Simply hear him or her out and then ask which of the questions he or she would like you to answer first.

Listening is an often overlooked component of communication success. Don't rush the person with whom you're talking, be aware of distractions, and pick up on subtle clues. By doing so, you'll have an enormous advantage in communicating well.

CHAPTER 22

BODY LANGUAGE

It's a scenario with which most experienced interviewers are quite familiar. You enter the lobby to meet your ten o'clock appointment. The candidate stands up, puts out a limp, somewhat soggy hand to shake, and intently stares at your feet. No matter how impressive the applicant's résumé, your impression of him or her has just sunk. Unfortunately, many people don't realize how important their facial expressions and body language are in the overall impression they create. If their body language contradicts what their mouths are saying, their credibility suffers. The old saying, "It's not what you say, but how you say it" is especially true when it comes to interacting with people successfully.

Understanding how your mannerisms affect how you are perceived is especially important if you are the least bit interested in career progression. It's a subject that's particularly important if you've been the victim of a layoff or downsizing. Losing your job is a traumatic experience, and it can shake the confidence of even the most self-assured worker. You may appear downbeat and depressed without even realizing how you are coming across. A simple thing such as smiling rather than frowning can make an enormous difference. Consider participating in a video-taped "mock interview" prior to going out on the real thing. Seeing yourself on tape can help you eliminate distracting or negative body language, and this information is invaluable in many settings—not just interviews.

Your body language can help or hurt you from the opening moments of a meeting.

The Handshake

You've probably done it thousands of times and scarcely thought about it. Although it's as natural as saying hello, your handshake says more about you than you might imagine.

Why is a handshake so important? Not only is it your first (and perhaps only) physical contact with another person, it largely dictates what type of first impression you make. In fact, it may play more of a role than any other single factor. While you may not remember the last time you received a really great handshake, you probably do remember the bad ones. How many times have you run across these characters?

- **Marvin the Muscular.** Actually he usually looks wimpy, like Wally Cox. He's intent on bringing you to your knees with a bone-crushing grip.

- **Princess Priscilla.** She daintily grasps the first joint of your proffered hand and wiggles her fingers up and down.

- **Dick the Fish.** He might have had his hand in a bucket of water—cold, clammy, slippery, and lifeless. Feels like you're touching something that should have a hook in its mouth.

Actually, the best handshake should be unobtrusive. You shouldn't remember it much one way or the other. Your handshake, like all other aspects of social etiquette shouldn't be left to chance, and a little practice never hurts. So think of this as Handshake 101. Hold your hand up in front of you. The area between the knuckles of your thumb and forefinger is called the web of your hand. The web of your hand should connect with the web of the hand of the person you're greeting. Miss that mark, and you'll feel that your handshake is slightly off.

What should you strive for? Ideally, your handshake should be firm, using the proper amount of pressure. It should represent you as a person of self-confidence who is socially mature. It also should be appropriately enthusiastic but with no excessive arm motion. Pumping the other person's arm down and back once is the proper amount of motion and shows you are glad to see him or her.

When you think about it, we certainly do shake hands a lot. It's an integral part of the American culture, so it's beneficial to learn how to do it well. We shake hands when we meet someone *and* when we say goodbye. Handshakes are appropriate when you congratulate someone on winning an award, getting an article published, or delivering a talk. However, there are also numerous occasions when it's inappropriate to shake hands—the most common being when the other person's hands are full. This often occurs at cocktail parties when the person you're greeting is balancing a plate of hors d'oeuvres in one hand and a beverage in the other. In this situation, a shoulder-high wave of the hand, along with the comment, "I can see your hands are full, but I did want to say hello," will suffice.

As our society becomes increasingly informal, the problem of who should offer to shake hands first has become much less important. Most of the time it doesn't make a bit of difference if you offer your hand first or vice versa. Of course, you should use common sense. If there is a dignitary, celebrity, or high-level politician in the room, you'd look a little silly and pushy if you ran up with your hand extended to introduce yourself. From a practical standpoint, most of us just aren't at enough parties with high-ranking dignitaries for this to be a real problem. The old custom of waiting for a woman to extend her hand is just that—an old custom. Men shouldn't be reticent to initiate the contact. Men shake women's hands, women shake men's, men shake men's, and women shake women's. Handshaking is a completely nonsexist activity.

One thing to keep in mind when you are at a social gathering is to make an effort to shake your host's hand when you arrive and when you leave. Proper etiquette dictates that you don't dally with other guests too long before finding and greeting your host. On leaving the gathering you should attempt to shake hands with your host as you say goodbye. Sometimes this is difficult, or you may feel uncomfortable if the host is obviously engaged in conversation. In these situations, it's perfectly acceptable for you to leave and either telephone or write a note expressing your thanks the next day.

Occasionally, you may hold out your hand only to have it ignored. Although this is embarrassing, the other person isn't normally being intentionally rude; they usually just didn't see your hand. If a couple of seconds go by and it's apparent that no handshake is forthcoming, casually drop your hand to your side. Yes, you'll feel uncomfortable doing so, but it's only a minor embarrassment and will soon pass.

Now, what if you don't naturally have a firm, dry handshake? Everyone suffers from times when their hands tend to be a little clammy. Unfortunately, these occasions always seem to occur when they're about to meet someone really important. Here are a couple of tips you might try to alleviate the more common problems:

- If your hands tend to be cold, try putting your right hand in your coat pocket or under you leg if you're seated. Make sure you don't hold cold beverages in your right hand, since this only exacerbates the problem.

- If you suffer from clammy hands, wiping the palm of your hand on your pant leg or skirt can help. It may take a little practice, but if you can master the move so as not to draw attention to it, the problem of clammy hands quickly goes away.

People, fairly or unfairly, judge you by your handshake. Many individuals will make a rough assessment of your career potential based solely on the firmness and dryness of your handshake. Keep these hints in mind, and your handshake won't be a hindrance to your career success.

Correct Seating

When meeting a business associate in his or her office or going in for an interview, it is important to know where to sit. Avoid sofas or other soft furniture; you'll have a tendency to sink into them, and they are often quite difficult to get out of. Instead, choose a standard hard-backed business chair. Sit with you lower back firmly against the back of the chair, leaning slightly forward. This give the impression of assertiveness and self-confidence. Place your briefcase or other materials on the floor next to your chair, not on the desk. This is perceived as being too forward and invading the other person's space.

Many people feel uncomfortable if the person with whom they are speaking is closer than 15 inches, so make sure you maintain the proper social distance. Your common sense will normally tell you when you are getting too close.

Eye Contact

Eye contact is one of the most important aspects of body language. If you don't look another person in the eye, it's tough to establish credibility. Conversely, never taking your eyes off him or her won't work either. One method to maintain the proper level of eye contact is to look a person in the eye when he or she is speaking, look away while you collect your thoughts or formulate your answer, then look back when you deliver your answer. Whenever you look at the other person, make sure you look him or her in the eye. Looking at his or her shoulder or ear is just as bad as not looking at him or her at all.

Understanding body language can help you determine how a business encounter is going. If the other person is nodding as you speak, this is generally a sign of approval. Crossed arms, fingers drumming on the desk, or paper-shuffling is a clear sign that you are losing your audience and need to make adjustments quickly.

Your body language can either support or contradict what you're saying. Taking steps to ensure you're coming across in a positive, self-confident manner is a good investment.

CHAPTER 23

REMEMBERING NAMES

Mention the term "social etiquette," and a lot of people have images of debutante parties and formal fancy dress balls. However, knowing how to behave in a variety of social situations is becoming increasingly important. This is particularly true for businesspeople who need to make the right first impression with contacts, prospects, and interviewers. You don't want to sabotage a hard-won meeting or interview with some social gaffe or get off on the wrong foot with a new client because of an etiquette faux pas. The issue of remembering people's names is a perfect example.

Trying to bluff your way through an encounter by not using any name at all usually only points out that you can't recall the person's name. When you wind up in this situation, a better strategy is to say something such as, "You know, I feel embarrassed, but sometimes I can't even remember my own sister's name. . . ." The other person will bear you no ill will since forgetting names is a common human failing. Besides, the odds are they didn't remember your name either.

As a matter of fact, it's a good strategy to assume that others don't remember your names. Taking the initiative of introducing yourself to people who should know who you are can relieve many awkward encounters. It allows the person to respond with a hearty "Why Judy, you didn't think I'd forgotten your name, did you?" Of course he or she did, but your initiative saved an embarrassing moment from occurring.

Remembering other people's names takes practice, but it's a great skill to develop. Concentration is the key to imbedding a name in your short-term memory. Memory experts suggest that you repeat the name as you are introduced. "Nice to meet you, *Frank*." Try to find some sort of association that will help you recall the name. Some people are easier than others. A man named Charlie who has a moon-shaped face and a cowlick would be easy to associate with the comic strip character Charlie Brown. Other names, especially common ones such as Dave or Nancy, attached to individuals with no unique physical characteristics are more difficult. Another trick that is particularly effective if you're both seated is to ask for the person's business card. Laying it on the table in front of you allows you to glance at it discreetly.

If you know you've seen someone before but can't, for your life, remember his or her name, try saying, "I remember meeting you at the Policeman's Ball at the Marriott last summer. I'm Jake Thomspon." Chances are the person will be impressed that you remembered the meeting, even if you didn't remember his or her name.

Introducing one person to a group puts your ability to remember names to its most severe test. Not only do you have to get the names straight, you've also got to keep in mind that there is a protocol dictating who is introduced to whom. Fortunately, this protocol is rather straightforward and logical. A lesser or more junior person is always introduced *to* a more important or senior person. For example, a younger person is introduced to an older person, a junior executive to a senior executive. Generally, a peer in your company would be introduced to a peer in another company, and a fellow worker would be introduced to a customer or client.

As you make the introductions try to add something personal about each individual. This will help facilitate an initial conversation between the people you're introducing and serves as an aide in recall. For example, you may say, "Ralph, I want you to meet my sister Susan. She's on vacation from Harvard and is working as an intern at AT&T this summer. Susan, this is Dr. Ralph Gleason, chief of pathology at Chicago Baptist."

If you don't remember everything about a person, don't panic. This is a common problem that often occurs when you remember one last name and one first name but neither party's entire name. By incorporating information about a person's background you should be able to make it through the introduction with no one being the wiser. For instance, you might try, "Mr. Smedwick, I'd like you to meet my friend Jason, who's with First American. Jason, this gentleman, I'm pleased to tell you, manages the Krispy Guppy account for SnackWell foods."

Remembering names and handling the responsibility of introducing strangers is a mark of a socially adept individual. It takes a lot of hard work, but people love to have their names remembered and pronounced correctly. We all tend to respect and be impressed by those who have mastered this art.

CHAPTER 24

THE ART OF BEING POLITICALLY CORRECT

It used to be that "politically correct" meant you voted Republican and the other guy was the one who was politically incorrect. My, how times have changed. Today, even the term "guy" is viewed by some as a politically incorrect term.

Words

The whole concept of political correctness has gotten out of hand. Ultimately, the only way to have a completely sex-free, gender-free, racial-free, or bias-free language is, in effect, to make it content-free as well.

You can quickly become overwhelmed with the nuances and subtle differences between what is correct and incorrect. However, despite the silliness surrounding some of the issues of politically correct speech, there are some fundamental etiquette issues of which you need to be aware so you don't offend others inadvertently.

An increased sensitivity to language has come about largely due to the influence of the women's movement over the past 30 years. As the workforce changed to include an increasing number of females in the professional and managerial ranks, language that had been acceptable for generations fell out of favor. Women quite rightly took offense at being referred to as "girls" and "gals," while their male counterparts were almost always referred to as "men." Although this increase in sensitivity was long overdue, it brought with it some confusion over semantics issues—confusion that continues to this day.

Lots of men still have difficulty knowing which terms to use to refer to the different sexes. A generally good piece of advice is to use the balance beam approach. If you're going to refer to one sex in a statement make sure you also include a reference to the opposite sex as well. Thus, the term "ladies" goes with "gentlemen," "boys" with "girls," and "men" with "women."

While this advice can help in most situations, the changing landscape of sexually correct language has altered the meaning of some words altogether. One common example is the term "guys." As it is used today, "guys" refers to members of both genders. Conversely, the term "gal" has fallen completely out of use, except for those whose reading habits begin and end with the works of Damon Runyon.

In the past ten years, we've seen attempts to make language gender free. In some cases, this works pretty well. For example, we refer to those who serve passengers on commercial airlines as "flight attendants," rather than "stewardesses" or "stewards." Other times, it becomes a bit absurd as in forgoing the terms "waitress" or "waiter" for the gender-neutral term "waitron." (Doesn't a picture of R2 D2 serving you coffee immediately spring to mind?)

All but the most ignorant of men now know that terms such as baby, sweetie, darling, or honey are likely to raise the ire of most women. Although these terms are still commonly used in the Southern states, it is interesting to observe that they are used by both sexes. A woman is just as likely to call a man "hon" as the reverse. Still, in a business setting, these terms are considered inappropriate.

Behavior

It wasn't all that long ago that old-fashioned chivalry was alive and well. Men were taught from a young age that they were expected to:

- open doors for a woman;

- light a woman's cigarette;

- walk on the outside of the sidewalk;

- stand up when a woman entered the room and remain standing until she sat down; and

- never shake a woman's hand unless she offers her hand first.

While most men viewed such behavior as simple politeness, women viewed many of these gestures as inappropriate, especially in a business setting.

The rules today are more straightforward and actually make more sense. Briefly, whoever would benefit from some assistance should receive it—regardless of sex. Chivalry isn't dead, it's just no longer based on gender. Take the following as examples:

- Whoever is going down the hall first should hold the door open for the person who follows.

- The person in the front of the elevator should get off first regardless of gender.

- Women should help men in putting their coat on if it's obvious they're having difficulty and vice versa.

- Whoever does the inviting for lunch picks up the tab regardless of sex or age.

- You rise when a person of either sex enters your office and remain standing until that person is seated.

Some people can become obsessed about using the right language or become paralyzed for fear of making an incorrect move. Most of these concerns have little foundation. Opt for gender-free language if you're given a choice; otherwise, don't worry about it. As long as you listen to your common sense and avoid the most blatantly sexist terms, you won't run into trouble.

CHAPTER 25

A PLACE FOR HUMOR

The prevailing opinion among humor consultants is that American business takes itself far too seriously. The fact that humor consultants actually exist indicates that some companies are taking the role of humor as a management tool seriously. It's certainly easy to understand why companies have become serious places to work. Increased competition, pressure to reduce costs, and the ever-present threat of layoffs puts a damper on light-hearted banter and jocularity. Company humor may seem to be an oxymoron in your workplace, however a noticeable trend is that appropriately applied humor can be good for both employees and business.

Business humor helps people take their work seriously without taking themselves too seriously. It enables them to laugh at the ironies and foibles that are a part of everyday life, and can help reduce the tensions so often found in today's work environment. Humor relaxes people and can be an effective component in team building. For example, a few years ago scientists at NASA were highly concerned that the Sky Lab spacecraft might actually crash to earth in a populated area with catastrophic consequences. Since scientists tend to be quite serious by nature, this increased sense of alarm caused much bickering and infighting. When Sky Lab harmlessly fell into the ocean, the question NASA management faced was how to recreate the environment of cooperation among scientists who were now barely speaking to each other. One manager came up with the idea of handing out t-shirts with a cartoon of Chicken Little and the words, ''I survived Sky Lab,'' emblazoned on it. These humorous t-shirts made the scientists realize they were taking themselves too seriously and served as an icebreaker in reuniting the team.

Consultants stress that humor in business has little to do with managers telling jokes. The problem with jokes is that what is funny to me may not be funny to you. Moreover, what is an inoffensive joke to one group of people may be viewed as insulting and insensitive by a different group. Finally, using jokes as an effective means of humor requires the ability to tell a joke well. Anyone who has been in the unfortunate position of having to tell a joke in front of a group of people can relate to how difficult the task truly is. Jokes are by and large a high-risk proposition for injecting humor into the workforce.

To look at how humor has been used most successfully in companies, it's interesting to observe some of the activities in the corporate training area. It didn't take trainers long to figure out that if some levity wasn't injected into the programs, such as "Statistics for the Nonquantitative Manager," few participants would return from the first break. An effective use of humor that began in one company's training area and spread throughout the organization involved the use of a potato. A particular training program on some dry subject depended on audience participation to be successful. To encourage involvement, the trainer gave a potato to individuals who made a particularly interesting point. The potatoes were completely unexpected and were greeted with much hilarity by the other members of the session. However, as the program continued and more potatoes were distributed as a reward for participation, the potato soon became a coveted object. Participants actually began to compete in order to be awarded a potato. This innovative use of humor increased audience involvement and directly contributed to the quality of the program. One manager who participated thought the potato would be a great way to increase involvement in his monthly staff meetings. The concept spread within the organization, and the potato finally became a motivational tool.

While the Protestant work ethic never included fun as one of its key objectives, humor can be an effective management force. The role of the fool as advisor to the king is an ancient tradition in which the fool provides valuable counsel through the use of humor. Humor enables the subordinate to address the leader on often sensitive subjects. Thus, the fool functions as an effective counterweight to the excessive pride and arrogance of the king. Modern advisors often find that couching their advice with a judicious amount of humor helps management accept negative feedback.

Finally, humor has the beneficial effect of relaxing people and improving the workforce's overall attitude. Since happy workers tend to be more productive, humor may be an underutilized managerial resource.

CHAPTER 26

WINNING TELEPHONE SKILLS

One of the most powerful weapons in your career arsenal is the telephone. However, even the most self-confident individual is prone to an outbreak of nerves when talking to a prospective client or employer on the phone. Often people feel they are intruding when they initiate a call or feel unprepared when they receive one. In this day of phone mail and answering machines, actually talking with a real human being sometimes becomes a challenge.

Since making a good impression on the phone is critical for career success, it is important to master the telephone:

- Although it seems obvious, you have to be heard in order to be effective on the phone. Tucking the phone under your chin or holding the receiver out of line with your mouth dramatically reduces the clarity and impact of your words. If you are soft-spoken, hold the phone directly in front of your mouth during your opening statement. There's no need to have the receiver under your chin during the first few seconds of your conversation.

- Have your opening statement prepared and practiced. There is a world of difference between thinking about how you will say something and actually articulating it. Practice by rehearsing with a friend or while driving in the car. Practicing will increase your self-confidence and the impact of your delivery. Your voice should project a pleasant personality without appearing timid or overly aggressive. Recording yourself on tape can help you learn how you come across.

- When making a cold call to a prospective customer, client, or employer, keep in mind that you are likely to have no more than five minutes to make your case. Thus, you want to make every statement count. Telephone sales pros suggest speaking for no more than 40 seconds at a time and pausing briefly after making an important point. An introductory statement might go like this: "Good morning, Mr. James. My name is Mark Wilson, and a mutual associate or ours, Jill Brown, thought my experience selling computers might be of benefit to your company. Is this a convenient time to talk?"

- One of the most common errors people make on the phone is failing to ask if the listener has time to talk. If the answer is no, ask when a convenient time would be to call the person back. Try to avoid having him or her call you back; this puts you in the uncomfortable situation of not knowing when the call will be returned.

- As much as you want to initiate rather than receive calls, being the recipient of a returned call is a fact of life. The problem is these calls come without any warning and can catch you by surprise. The carefully prepared opening remark flies out of your head as you frantically try to remember to whom you're talking and what aspect of your background you most wanted to discuss. A strategy to buy yourself time is the following: "Thanks very much for returning my call, Ms. Smith. Let me put you on hold for just a moment while I change phones." This tactic allows you to collect your thoughts or quickly review some notes made in anticipation of the call.

- Keeping track of everyone you've called can become unwieldy very quickly. The problem becomes worse if it is several days before you finally connect with your prospect. To keep your memory sharp, keep a detailed call list of everyone you're trying to contact. Update it daily so the names are quickly identifiable. Remember, you will only have a few seconds to "change phones," which doesn't give you a great deal of time to refresh your memory.

- People who sell products over the phone recommend that you tailor your speaking style to your listener. If he or she speaks quickly and directly, use short concise statements. Conversely, if your listener's style is relaxed and friendly, adopt a more informal tone.

Using Answering Machines

Answering machines are a fact of life. People loath listening to a long message, so keep your own recording brief and to the point: "Hello, you have reached 234-5555. I'm sorry I'm not here to take your call personally, but please leave a message at the tone and I'll return your call as soon as possible."

You want your phone message to be consistent with an image of quality and professionalism. Avoid cutesy prerecorded messages with a disco beat or the opening from Beethoven's Fifth Symphony. Similarly, this is not the place to have your four-year-old record his or her first phone message.

If you have the discipline to do it, recording a new greeting each day takes some of the impersonality out of answering machines. For example, "Hi, this is Catherine Miller. It's Monday, June 27, and I'll be out of the office this morning but will return in the early afternoon. Please leave your number and a brief message, and I'll get back to you just as soon as possible."

Make sure your answering machine can be accessed from a touch-tone phone. This is a common feature offered on most machines. Remember to check your machine on a regular basis throughout the day so you do return calls as quickly as possible.

When leaving a message on someone else's machine, explain why you are calling to ensure that your call is not mistaken for that of the ubiquitous mutual-fund salesperson. Try something like, "Good morning, this is Bill Marcus. I am following up on my letter of October 10, which was prompted by our mutual associate, Paula Jones. I can be reached at 234-5555 until five o'clock today or 235-7777 after six o'clock. I look forward to speaking with you soon."

Tenacity is critical for success in telephoning. Unfortunately the likelihood of your actually reaching your prospect on the first call is slim. "Telephone tag," while frustrating, is unavoidable. However, I have discovered when I have finally made the connection after repeated attempts, my caller often comments positively on my persistence. Never has a speaker indicated that they were put off by repeated messages. Thus, with the telephone, as with all aspects of the job search process, err on the side of assertiveness.

Other Technology

Answering machines often are being replaced by voice mail systems. Voice mail offers greater flexibility and is available to residential customers under the names like Memory Call. Remember, leaving a message rather than just your name and number can substantially reduce the amount of telephone tag you have to play.

Carrying a beeper ensures that you are immediately aware of incoming calls. A growing number of people now wear them as part of their day-to-day jobs, making the distinctive beeping less noticeable than it once was. However, the noise is sometimes an intrusion and should be considered when you decide whether to purchase one. If receiving calls quickly is important to you, you might consider leaving your beeper number on your answering machine message. This ensures that you're always available to clients and prospects.

CHAPTER 27

AIRLINE CONDUCT

You may not like the hassles of flying, but it beats traveling by wagon train. Many people are still amazed that jumbo jets can actually stay in the air, so the fact that the food is sometimes so-so isn't particularly surprising.

Anyone who travels on a regular basis knows that air travel is not perfect. Things go wrong. However, you can keep your blood pressure in a reasonable range if you remember that, when delays occur or problems ensue, *there's nothing you can do about it.* Quite frankly, unless you know how to fly the plane or fix it, there isn't much you can contribute to solving the problem, so you might as well sit back and relax. Granted, that's often easier said than done. That's one of the reasons travel advisors recommend that you always take along plenty to read. The trick is to bring not only business-related materials, but also something fun. It's a lot easier to wait out a delay if you can distract yourself with some enjoyable reading material. You'll also find that having lots to read tends to make the time go faster once you are finally in the air.

The basics of airline etiquette largely revolve around being sensitive to the needs of your fellow travellers. Satisfying your own needs at the expense of others is out-and-out rude. Unfortunately, air travel is characterized by a lot of people trapped in close proximity for an (often) extended period of time. In these circumstances, you sometimes behave in ways that you wouldn't otherwise. To keep this behavior to a minimum, observe the basics of airline etiquette, which include the following:

- The compartment above your seat is meant for your belongings and for belongings of other passengers seated in your row. Don't put your stuff in a compartment over row 15 when you're sitting in row 43.

- If an item can fit under the seat in front of you, put it there. Suitcases were meant to have your feet rest on top of them. Unless you travel exclusively by corporate jet, leave the alligator bag at home and invest in some "road warrior" luggage.

- It's amazing that so many otherwise smart people can't quite grasp the concept of "carry-on luggage is limited to two pieces." Now, most of us forgive Aunt Matilda who boards the plane at Christmas laden with gifts for her grandchildren. After all, who knows when she last flew, if ever? (Which is one reason most experienced travellers try to avoid flying during December.) However, it's inexcusable for the obviously experienced traveller to make the same gaffe. Fortunately, airlines seem to be cracking down on this problem, with some carriers actually measuring your bags before they allow you to board.

- As you board the plane remove your carry-on bag from your shoulder. Carrying a bulky bag on your back ensures that you will thunk the heads of all seated aisle passengers as you journey to your seat.

- Keep in mind the close proximity of a full airplane. A lot of the problems that generally occur come about when you forget this fact. Have you ever had the unpleasant experience of having a seatmate spread out a week's worth of newspapers when you're jammed together three to a row? Forgo the newspaper unless the seat next to you is unoccupied, or stick to magazines and books.

- Remember the saying, "Silence is golden," and be sensitive to whether the person sitting next to you wants to talk. Having your "How are you?" acknowledged with little more than a grunt is a sure signal that your seatmate want to be left alone.

- How about when you want to be left alone but don't want to be rude? Hold a pen in your hand when you're reading. This sends the message that the material is important and that your full concentration is required. Periodically underlining or placing check marks on the page reinforces this impression. Of course, this strategy works better when you're reading *The Wall Street Journal* and not the latest Steven King novel.

  Headphones can make it literally impossible for others to disturb you. You may use airline flights to listen to a variety of tapes for both pleasure and business. However, by simply placing the headphones on your head, without listening to anything, you send the message that you'd rather not talk. Airline headsets that plug into the console in the arm of your seat accomplish the same thing.

- Especially on longer flights, the call of nature can be loud and, eventually, impossible to ignore. By all means, try to avoid timing your trip to the restroom with the food and drink carts' progression down the aisle. It's virtually impossible to slide past the carts, so the only alternative is for either you or the cart to back up. Although the flight attendant will smile politely at you, you know what he or she is thinking. Remember your mother's admonishments from childhood; make sure you visit the facilities before embarking on the trip.

- Modern telecommunications have invaded space at 30,000 feet with air-linked telephone service now commonly offers on most jets. Air telephone etiquette revolved around two issues:

  1. Don't use the phone unless you absolutely have to. It is typically located in the back of the center seat which makes your use of it inconvenient to others unless you're sitting in the center seat. It's also impossible to conduct a telephone conversation without distracting those sitting around you.

  2. Don't shout. People have a tendency to shout into the phone because the muffled roar of the engines makes it impossible for them to hear what the other party is saying. However, they erroneously assume that since they're having difficulty hearing, the other party must also have the same problem. Actually, those on the ground can hear you just fine. A normal tone of voice will suffice nicely.

- The number one complaint among experienced business travellers involves reclining seats. Just because your seat reclines doesn't mean you have to take advantage of this feature. Actually, most business traveller wish the seats didn't recline at all. Unfortunately, when one person reclines his or her seat, a domino effect takes place throughout the plane. If you recline your seat, remember that it makes it very difficult for the person behind you to continue to do any work. This is especially true if he or she is trying to work on a laptop computer. It's also virtually impossible for passengers to reach under the seat in front of them if that seat is fully reclined.

  If the person in front of you does push their seat all the way back, there's nothing inappropriate about politely asking them to bring their seatback forward. Try a statement such as, "I hate to disturb you, but it's a little tight back here. I was wondering if you would mind bringing your seat forward a little bit?" It's a rare individual who feels entitled to recline his or her seat at the expense of the person sitting behind him or her. Your request usually will be graciously fulfilled.

Finally, a word about dressing for an airline trip. Not too many years ago, travelling on an airplane was akin to going to church: Everyone got decked out in their finest outfits. Although those days appear to be long gone, it's a mixed blessing. Wearing a suit or dress on a plane, if you don't have a business meeting when you arrive, doesn't make a great deal of sense—unless you're someone who just likes to dress up. The etiquette of business travel attire is that you should always look neat and professional. Freshly pressed slacks with a blouse or shirt, and blazer is an acceptable and comfortable travelling ensemble for both men and women. However, unless the flight is a vacation charter, people wearing shorts or a shirt with no sleeves shouldn't be allowed to board.

Etiquette on an airline is mostly about sensitivity to others. Remember that the environment is unique. The normal territorial social distance between people shrinks from 15 inches down to 6. Things that wouldn't be irritating if you had more space become bothersome given the confinement of the plane.

CHAPTER 28

STAYING IN HOTELS

Hotel living—love it or loath it, but there's no getting around that it is a fact of life for the modern business professional. Hotel living is similar in some ways to staying at your parents' house. There are rules of etiquette, which if followed, make the visit more enjoyable and less stressful.

Although the world "hotel" may conjure up images of luxury, the experienced traveller knows this is not necessarily the case. Certainly, the opportunity to stay at a five-star hotel enables most of us to experience a lifestyle somewhat more grandiose than what we are used to back home. Conversely, spending a week at the No-Name Motel can make you wonder what prior sins you're now atoning for.

Check-In

Normally, this goes without a hitch. Experienced travellers know they must be prepared to present their credit card to the front desk clerk even if their account is being billed direct to a company. You can expedite the check-in process by having your card out and ready before you get to the front desk. Nothing is more frustrating to people behind you than to watch you fumble around for your wallet when you've been standing in line for 15 minutes.

A fact of life is that periodically you are likely to have some sort of problem with your reservation. When this occurs (and it will), the most important point is not to lose your temper. Remember that the only person who may be able to help you is the individual behind the desk. Although it may make you feel better to start screaming at this person, it makes little sense from a practical standpoint.

If your reservation has been lost or the hotel is over-booked, the first thing hotel personnel will attempt to do is verify that you did indeed have a reservation. Thus, make sure you keep your confirmation number handy. The easiest way to do this is to have your travel agent include in on your itinerary. The hotel's willingness to accommodate you will depend on how obligated they feel toward you. The confirmation number goes a long way toward establishing your credibility.

Sometimes the hotel will automatically upgrade you to a nicer room on a nicer floor if the regular rooms are sold out. If they don't volunteer to do this, ask them if there is anything available on their concierge floor. Don't be shy about asking. Although you don't want to needlessly berate the poor person behind the desk, you do want to be assertive in suggesting the various options that may be available. People who ask for things get more than those who don't.

If the hotel is, in fact, completely booked, they will attempt to find you accommodations nearby. While this is a hassle, it beats sleeping on the street. Again, it's important not to vent your frustration at the desk clerk. This person's range of influence is usually quite limited. All the desk clerk can normally do is attempt to find you a place to lay your tired head. Lambasting him or her about the inefficiencies of the hotel's reservation system won't do you a lot of good. However, before you leave, make sure you get the name of the hotel's general manager. This is the person who can actually make amends if he or she is approached in the right way.

Unfortunately, since it's usually evening when you're checking in, this person has long since gone off duty. In seeking compensation for your inconvenience, the pen is mightier than the voice. After you have returned from your trip, write the general manager a polite but forceful note. Outline the specifics of what occurred and express your displeasure. Mentioning that you are a frequent visitor to the hotel, or a member of one of their "frequent guest" programs never hurts. There's no need to ask for specific compensation. Mention your disappointment in the hotel and express your hope that you can be influenced to use the services of the hotel again in the future. You are likely to be pleasantly surprised with the reply you receive.

A classic example from my own experience occurred when my wife and I were vacationing in Cancún, Mexico. Upon arriving at the hotel, we were informed that it was overbooked and that we would be put up in a comparable hotel nearby. Although this was disappointing since the original hotel was one of our favorites, we graciously took their offer along with the free drink and dinner coupons that were made available. Once we were back home, my wife decided to write a letter to the general manager expressing her disappointment in the hotel's reservation system. Lo and behold, three months later we got a letter from the general manager offering us three free nights at the hotel. We subsequently took advantage of this offer and received the red carpet treatment. I'll never forget a waiter arriving at our cabana carrying a large chocolate chip cookie inscribed with the words, "Welcome back Mark & Karen."

Thus, the first rule of hotel etiquette is not to lose your cool. If something goes wrong, make sure you obtain the name of the person in charge of the hotel and follow up with a polite but firm letter as soon as you return home. Fortunately, most of the time your room will be ready for you when you arrive, and check-in will proceed smoothly.

The Hotel Restaurant

If the purpose of your trip is an interview and the city if unfamiliar to you, a good piece of advice is to limit your dining to the hotel restaurant or coffee shop. Yes, the prices in these establishments are higher than you might pay otherwise, but the cost is offset by the fact that you know you won't get lost travelling back and forth to dinner. Besides, most companies know what prices to expect if you're eating in the hotel and, while it will seem expensive to you, it won't to them.

If you're travelling by yourself, there is no reason you should feel obligated to eat in your room. Many people, especially women, sometimes feel uncomfortable going to a restaurant and asking for a table for one. Fortunately, this feeling of discomfort is largely just in your head. Hotel dining rooms actually expect that a large percentage of their customers will be businesspeople travelling by themselves. As an increasing number of women have entered the workforce, a woman dining by herself doesn't attract the attention it once did.

A helpful tip in increasing your comfort level when dining alone is to bring something to read with you, such as files to review, or the newspaper or a book. Having some sort of reading material can make the experience all the more pleasurable.

Spending Company Money Wisely

The cardinal rule when on the road, either at the behest of your employer or for an interview, is to treat the company's money like your own. Most companies don't expect you to subsist on Spam sandwiches, but they aren't going to subsidize a lobster dinner. Discretion and good judgment should be your watchwords. If you enjoy a cocktail before or after dinner, pay for it with cash or put the tab on your personal credit card. Employers increasingly are taking a look at what people are charging when they're on the road. This is especially true if you're travelling for an interview. A large lounge bill or charges for multiple in-room movies send the wrong message.

A few more words on in-room movies. First, you got to ask yourself, "Can I really justify shelling out $8.95 to watch *The Karate Kid IV?*" Virtually no company will reimburse you for the movie, and you want to be careful about the impression you make. If you're in town for an interview, you can bet that someone back at the office will take at least a quick glance at your bill to see if any unusual charges pop up. Stick with watching a ballgame or sitcom reruns.

Tipping

Staying at a large hotel for any extended length of time brings you into contact with a variety of hotel employees, many of whom wouldn't mind being compensated for their services. The etiquette of hotel tipping is often confusing, but here are some general guidelines that may be of help. While these guidelines apply specifically to larger hotels, you'll meet many of the same people in all but the smallest establishments. Recommended amounts to tip are based on hotel service in larger cities. You can tip less in smaller towns. However, the cardinal rule in tipping is don't ever feel obligated. If the individual is surly or the service sub-standard, don't feel obligated to tip.

When your cab pulls up to the front of the hotel, you will be greeted by the *doorman*, who will take your bags to the front desk. Depending on the amount of luggage you have, tip this person $1 to $5. You would give him a similar tip for his assistance in getting your bags into the cab when you depart.

The *bellman* will transport your bags from the lobby to your room. Don't feel obligated to use his services if you only have a carry-one bag or single suitcase. Five dollars is appropriate in most instances; give $10 if you're travelling with your family and have a large amount of luggage being transported to your room.

If the air conditioning doesn't work, the television goes on the blink, or some other mechanical problem occurs, tip the *engineer* who comes to fix it between $2 to $5 depending on his or her promptness, efficiency, and politeness.

The *concierge* usually found in larger hotels can be a marvelous resource on everything from dinner reservations to obtaining tickets to sold-out events. Don't hesitate to avail yourself of his or her services because he or she really can help you have a marvelous stay in a new city. A tip of $2 to $10 (or more, if he or she can get you decent seats to the Final Four) is appropriate depending on the difficulty of the service.

The *parking attendant* who gets your car from the garage should get $1 to $2 per trip. You don't need to tip anything when you drop off the car at valet parking.

Even though a 15 percent gratuity is tacked onto the already expensive *room service* bill, it's good etiquette to tip the person who brings you the food an additional $2. At many hotels, this person doesn't get the entire 15 percent, and that extra money can help accelerate future room service deliveries.

Regardless of the ritziness of your accommodations, you should tip the *cleaning woman* who takes care of your room. Don't leave the tip each day, but leave $2 per night at the end of your stay. Some hotels provide envelopes specifically for this purpose. If there's no envelope, leave the tip in the bathroom or on your pillow.

To ease yourself through the process of hotel tipping, it's a good idea to make sure you carry a number of dollar bills with you. Remember, tipping should be a token of appreciation for serviced rendered. As mentioned before, never feel obligated to tip if the level of service is sub-standard.

Doing Business in a Hotel

You read increasingly about the "virtual office." For an increasing number of businesspeople, their office happens to be wherever they are. If you're on the road a lot, that means your office is likely to be your hotel room. Hotels are taking different approaches to this phenomenon. Large hotels, especially those located in major cities that cater primarily to businesspeople, are adapting their services more and more to meet the needs of this group. Other chains unfortunately are taking a head-in-the-sand approach and offering few, if any, additional services. Your choice of where you stay may well be influenced by the business services that the hotel offers.

When you check in, ask about the availability of fax machines and whether you'll be able to hook your computer modem into the hotel's communication system. Also, inquire about telephone access and whether you can use a carrier other than the service with which the hotel contracts. You'll normally be able to use your own long-distance carrier, but you may have to dial a fairly long number in order to access the service. However, your patience and willingness to dial these extra numbers is more than offset by the financial savings you gain by avoiding the hotel's direct-dial rate.

One tip to avoid entering a 17-digit code for each call is to press the pound key after you complete a call, rather than hanging up. By pressing the pound key for two seconds, you'll get a dial tone enabling you to make your next call. Another benefit of this trick is that hotels normally charge you up to $1 every time you place a call. By pressing the pound key after each call, you can avoid separate charges.

Along with using your hotel room as a personal office, it may become a place in which you conduct meetings. Using your room in this fashion has its own set of business etiquette rules.

Ideally, if you'll be conducting a meeting in your room, you'll want a suite. However, in these days of cost cutting and belt tightening, that may not be possible. If it's not, you'll want to take the proper steps to ensure your hotel room reflects the proper business image.

- Make sure all personal items are stored away. Remove your toilet items from the bathroom counter and place them either in your luggage or in a drawer that can be closed. It's also a good idea to remove those items that scream out the fact you're in a hotel room. These include the pay-per-movie card on top of the television, hotel flyers, and other clutter.

- Make sure there are enough chairs for everyone. No one will feel comfortable sitting on the bed, which of course should be made before the meeting. If the proper number of chairs won't comfortably fit in your room, it's a sign that you need a larger space. Most hotels have a variety of meeting rooms, usually at reasonable prices, that may be a more viable option than conducting the meeting in your room. If you're a paying guest of the hotel you may find that you can negotiate a very reasonable rate for the use of one of these conference rooms.

- If the meeting is one-on-one and involves a member of the opposite sex, this adds an extra element of sensitivity to meeting in your room. Although it may sound silly, you might consider keeping the door ajar, especially if this is your first meeting. As long as the maid isn't vacuuming the room, this gesture will raise the comfort level for both of you and allow you to focus quickly on the business at hand.

If you're on the interview trail, it's very common for some interviews to take place in a hotel room. The etiquette of interviewing in a hotel is similar to interviewing in a person's office. Once you arrive, call from the lobby to let the recruiter know that you've arrived. Once you're in his or her room, focus on the person with whom you're meeting and don't become distracted by any unique feature of the room. Aside from those differences, an interview in a hotel doesn't differ from an interview in any other location.

Although everyone misses the creature comforts of home, hotel living does have its advantages. After all, someone does come in every day to clean up your room. Becoming knowledgeable about the etiquette of hotel stays can make your visit all the more enjoyable.

CHAPTER 29

WATCHING YOUR TABLE MANNERS

John thought he had the account in the bag. In fact, he nearly did. As a last step before finalizing the deal, Ms. Igor invited John and his wife out to dinner. Unfortunately, John decided this would be the perfect time to experiment with snails. If the snails had arrived in a puff pastry shell, everything would have been fine. However, they arrived in their shells accompanied with a variety of tools which John had no earthly idea how to operate. His attempt to appear "suave and sophisticated" blew up around his ears with disastrous results.

It used to be assumed that everyone learned good table manners as they were growing up. While that may never have really been the case, it is apparent that a smaller percentage of us are receiving the basic grounding in table manners than previous generations. As our society has become increasingly informal and busy, these basic skills are often no longer taught at home. Since college years are not usually distinguished by a plethora of fine dining experiences, it's not uncommon for young professionals to be thrust into the business world with little awareness for what they should and shouldn't do in a formal dining situation.

Throughout your life, you will have numerous opportunities to advance (or derail) your career over a meal. Thus, proper table manners are an important skill to learn. Fortunately, the rules aren't as complex as they might seem. You'll find a knowledge of dining etiquette comes in handy when you're at a formal dinner party or dining in a first-class restaurant. Once you've mastered the basics, you'll feel more self-confident and stop worrying about whether you're making some sort of social blunder.

Observing what others do is perhaps the easiest way to pick up the basics. When the soup is served, observe which spoon the person across the table from you picks up. In a worst case scenario, you can always ask the person sitting next to you. Don't worry about appearing unsophisticated.

However, there's no excuse for making a less than favorable impression because of bad manners.

Basic Table Etiquette

Take your clue from your host about when to start eating. Either watch him or her out of the corner of your eye, or don't start eating until the majority of your dining companions have started. Remember that this rule holds true for each course that is served. You don't start on your salad until your host begins eating, nor do you start on the main course until after your host takes the first bite.

The time to start eating at a buffet party is a little different. Ideally, you'll be able to join a table with other guests who are already seated. The general rule is to wait until there are three or more guests at the table before starting to eat. Of course, don't leave your common sense at home. If you are the second to the last person in the buffet line, don't deny yourself food just because your table didn't muster a quorum.

It's sometimes the little things—like napkins—that cause us the most discomfort. Unfold your napkin entirely the moment you sit down. If the napkin is extra large, fold it in half. If it still covers your shoes, you've been given a tablecloth. This is usually indicative of a newly opened establishment or a weird sense of humor on the part of your host. If you have to leave the table during the meal, don't put your napkin on the table; it's considered an affront to the other guests. Also, don't take it with you. Simply leave it on your chair. When dinner is over and everyone gets up to leave place your napkin on the table (not on your plate).

It's actually OK to put your elbows on the table, although it's hard to believe Mom and Dad were wrong. Before the meal and while dinner is being served you should rest only your wrists on the table. However, between courses or at the end of the meal, it's socially acceptable to put your elbows on the table.

You can tell a lot about what you'll be eating by observing how the silverware is set up. Two tips to keep in mind as you're deciding which utensil to use: Eat from the outside in; and, when in doubt, peek at your neighbor.

Let's explain "eating from the outside in." Generally, a formal dinner place setting will look like this: From left to right you will have little fork, big fork, plate, big knife, little knife, and spoon. You will use the utensils on the outside first and progress to those closer to your plate. For example, the smaller fork to your far left is for the salad, which will be served first. The larger fork is for the main course. The plate actually isn't used for anything. This ornamental plate will be removed shortly before the main course and replaced with a similar plate with food on it. The large knife to the right of the plate is for your main course. The smaller knife to its right is for the salad or cheese course that precedes it. Any flatware set above the plate is for dessert. A fork above the knife indicates you'll be served pie or cake, whereas a single spoon above your plate indicates the eventual arrival of ice cream or pudding.

Sooner or later you probably will be confronted by the finger bowl. Finger bowls are most common in New England since they originated there. Originally used as a precursor to Wet-Naps, finger bowls most commonly accompany fish dishes such as lobster, clams, or oysters. The purpose of the finger bowl is to give you an opportunity to clean the tips of your fingers. Not very helpful you say? Well, you're right. Which explains why finger bowls are falling out of fashion. However, should you be in Kennebunkport after a fine lobster dinner, you'll be prepared.

In a restaurant, you need to be alert to the signals waiters look for to determine when you're done with your meal. You communicate with your waiter by where you place your silverware on your plate. For example, when you're taking a momentary pause in eating, you place your fork and knife angled inward from the lower right and left outer rims of the plate, forming an inverted V. This tells the waiter you are not finished with your meal. When you are done, place your fork and knife next to each other pointed toward the top of the plate. An alternative signal is to place the utensils together horizontally across the plate.

You've faced this next problem at one time or another. You don't want to swallow something you've already put in your mouth, such as a tough piece of meat or an olive pit. Raising your napkin to your mouth and transferring the object to it is acceptable as long as you don't draw attention to yourself. Strict social etiquette calls for you to bring your fork to your mouth and place the object on the fork with your tongue. This is reputed to be the most socially acceptable method since the fork-to-mouth movement is a common one. However, most people find this more difficult, since it requires more physical skill to use a fork than a napkin.

What foods can you eat with your hands? In many cases, it will depend on whether you're eating inside or outside. For example, food such as corn on the cob, spare ribs, and hamburgers are staples of the informal, outdoor get-together and should be picked up. It's actually considered improper to serve the first two items indoors unless it's an extremely informal affair.

Eat your soup by dipping the spoon away from yourself. This makes it less likely that you'll spill liquid on your shirt. It's OK to pick up the soup bowl or cup and drink the broth after you've eaten the vegetables or other solid ingredients.

Given the increased pace of business life, more and more people lunch at their desks. While ten years ago eating at your desk was frowned on at many companies, today it has become the norm at many of these same organizations. Keep two thoughts in mind. First, never bring food that emanates a strong odor back to your office. Not only is it likely to be offensive to those who sit near you, but the smell will tend to linger throughout the day. Those grilled onions may have been delicious at noon, but you'll hardly find them terribly appealing at four o'clock. Second, dispose of drink containers when you are finished with your meal. We sometimes have a tendency to let cans of soda and cups of cold coffee accumulate like a small army. If you haven't finished that soda within 15 minutes of your meal, you probably never will. Put it in the trash (or empty it and put it in the recycling bin) before you inadvertently knock it over.

A final point to remember about table etiquette is that embarrassing situations happen. If you make a mistake, don't draw attention to it and you'll find that no one else will notice.

Part Four

CAREER TRANSITIONS AND ALTERNATIVES

CHAPTER 30

TIPS FOR LAYOFF SURVIVORS

They called it "Black Friday"—the day when layoff announcements would be made. By noon, the winners and losers had been identified. However, once the news began to sink in, who was who became more difficult to determine. Ironically, you may not necessarily be one of the lucky ones if you survive a layoff.

Of course, if you still have a job you have much to be thankful for. A regular paycheck and company benefits are nothing to take lightly. Although there is no minimizing the trauma of losing your job, laid-off workers often voice a feeling of relief that the decision has finally been made. Since layoffs are often preceded by months of rumors, career counselors state that individuals are typically glad to end the uncertainty, even if the result is termination.

The same cannot be said for those who are left behind. If you are a layoff survivor, you must adapt your behavior to new realities. Some survivors emerge from this period of change in stronger positions, while others only alienate co-workers and supervisors and become prime candidates for the next round of downsizing. Emory Mulling, president of the outplacement firm The Mulling Group, emphasizes that you must make an extra effort to be as outwardly positive as possible. This is often difficult, especially since a friend of yours may have been laid off. Your feelings toward your company are likely to be quite negative, and you may find yourself bad-mouthing your employer. This can be career suicide. Remember, corporations don't enjoy laying off workers. It's a decision driven by financial necessity.

Make sure you keep your negative thoughts to yourself. Although you may feel diminished loyalty to the company, if you play your cards correctly, you may actually increase your career potential. Management realizes that layoffs and reorganizations are difficult to everyone. Those people who maintain a positive attitude are likely to stand out. As difficult as it may

141

be, if you are outwardly enthusiastic and strive to be perceived as a team player, your stock is likely to rise in your boss's eyes.

Mr. Mulling also points out that you'll probably have a new boss as a result of the reorganization. Adapting to a new boss is always a challenge. One key to getting off on the right foot is to pay attention to communication styles. Some bosses like to communicate by memo; others prefer verbal exchanges. Be alert to which format your new boss prefers and adjust your style accordingly.

Dr. Carol Beavers, senior vice-president with the outplacement and career management firm EnterChange Inc., says to be ready for an increase in your workload. Someone has to perform the tasks previously handled by others, and it's likely you'll be tapped for additional duties if you're a layoff survivor. At this point, you can either resist the changes or support the new management. Despite what you may be feeling in your heart, your career will be best served by a pragmatic approach to your current situation. If you cling to the old ways, refuse to shoulder your share of the new workload, or are perceived as a malcontent, your name will go to the head of the list should future layoffs become necessary.

Both Mr. Mulling and Dr. Beavers concur that you should use this time to take a realistic assessment of your career. Despite all your efforts and regardless of how well you are perceived by your employer, you may not survive the next round of layoffs. Employers are often unwilling or unable to discuss their future personnel plans. This makes being realistic about your long-term survival all the more important. Although this is simple logic, few individuals want to initiate a job search. What psychologists refer to as denial, "it won't happen to me," unfortunately can have disastrous consequences. If your research and the all-important internal company network indicates that more layoffs are likely, use the time beforehand to your advantage. Take the initiative to update your résumé, contact executive recruiters, and check out your options.

Succeeding as a layoff survivor requires an awareness of the new realities, keeping your frustrations to yourself, and assessing which way the winds of the future are blowing. Play your cards right and your career might actually benefit from this traumatic time.

CHAPTER 31

HELPING A SPOUSE WHO HAS LOST A JOB

Helping your spouse when he or she loses a job is difficult. You want to help but may be uncertain about what to do. Since you can't conduct the job search for them, you may feel powerless to assist. New tensions begin to creep into even the best of relationships. Questions asked out of love and concern can often be interpreted as intrusive and unwelcome. Supporting your spouse through this difficult time requires both compassion and understanding.

In this age of two-income families, when one spouse loses a job, it can cause financial panic. It's a good idea to sit down as soon as possible and examine your family's budget. Although it's prudent to defer nonessential major purchases, don't go overboard and cut out all of your social and recreational activities. That will only put more strain on your relationship. Once they've reviewed their budget, most families discover their financial pressures are not as great as they originally anticipated.

Surviving as a couple depends on keeping the lines of communication open. This is often more difficult than it sounds. Although you will naturally be interested in how your spouse's job search is going, you don't want to make your questions sound like an inquisition. There is a fine line between too little and too much interest. You want to make your spouse feel comfortable in discussing both the highs and lows of the job search. Asking questions such as, "Is there anything I can do to help?" sets the right tone and shows your spouse you sincerely care.

If the job search drags on for a number of months, you may find yourself becoming skeptical about how hard your spouse is looking for work. You need to remember that no one can devote 100 percent of their time to their job search. People need opportunities to relax and forget about the pressure of finding new employment. It's very important not to criticize your spouse when he or she pursues leisure activities. If your spouse senses that you disapprove, he or she is likely to withdraw. This will only serve to raise the level of tension between you.

Psychologists who specialize in family counseling believe that men and women react differently to being out of work. Despite society's changing attitude toward traditional male and female roles, many men still feel they bear the primary responsibility for providing for their families. Men also tend to define their self-image by the type of work they perform and often find it more difficult than women to discuss being out of work.

Women face different issues when they find themselves suddenly unemployed. Many women sacrificed traditional female roles in order to achieve business success, so they may have difficulty justifying past choices. A husband needs to be sure he doesn't downplay the importance of his wife's career. Statements like, "That's OK, we really don't need the money," can be well intentioned, but they backfire. The wife may interpret these remarks as minimizing the decisions she has made in her life.

The best way for you to survive a job loss as a couple is to realize that it is an event that affects both of you. It is very difficult for one spouse to work hard at the office all day and then come home and be a cheerleader. Many of us want time to decompress and relax when we leave work. The last thing we want to do is talk. However, you may be the first live person your spouse has seen all day. Even though you may desire peace and quiet, your spouse is likely to crave human interaction.

If the pressures become too great, don't overlook the value a qualified psychologist or marriage counselor can provide. Seeking professional help is not an admission of weakness. Having an impartial third party to whom you can vent frustrations can be enormously beneficial.

Helping your spouse through the loss of a job puts pressure on even the most stable of marriages. The key to success is remembering that marriage is a partnership. If you work together during this difficult time, you are likely to discover that your relationship is stronger once the ordeal is over.

CHAPTER 32

MOVING TO A NEW LOCATION

჻჻჻

The New Job

When you're considering a job offer in a new town, make sure you take the time to find out how much your new paycheck you'll actually get to keep. Salary is one thing, what you can buy with it is often a completely different matter. For example, make sure you know about city and state income taxes in order to determine exactly how much you'll bring home. Folks who live in Florida and Texas, which have no state income tax, enjoy a higher standard of living on the same dollars than their counterparts in Boston or New York.

The cost of staples, such as gasoline, varies enormously from state to state and can eat up a large chunk of your paycheck. Gasoline that cost $1 per gallon in Atlanta can cost over $1.25 in Los Angeles or Miami. This can add up quickly if you have a long commute. People also often overlook factors such as parking when they compare salary offers. If you rent or purchase a condominium, parking may not be included in your monthly rent or mortgage. In some major cities, you'll need another $300 per month to have handy access to your car. You'll also want to ask your employer about parking at work. Employer-paid parking is a great perk since it's usually not taxed as income.

The best way to evaluate the true cost of working in a particular city is to visit for two to three days. To comparison shop effectively, the first step is to get a copy of the city's major newspaper. Check out rental and housing prices. Call an insurance agent and find out how much your new insurance policies (rental, auto, and so on) will cost. Call the utility companies to find out what the rates are and what an average customer pays. Although the rate may be higher, your actual costs might go down. For example, rates are fairly high in southern California, but because of the temperate climate, people actually wind up using less electricity. Conversely, residents in colder climates may have gas heat at low rates because they use a lot of it.

A variety of services publish cost-of-living information for cities nation-wide. Ask the research librarian at your public library for a report. The *National Business Employment Weekly* also publishes cost-of-living data approximately once a month. You can find it on newsstands or in the placement office of your local university.

The data in these reports can often appear contradictory. Although no report will list New York or Los Angeles among the nation's cheapest places to live, estimates vary widely on the actual cost of living in different cities. This is because the statisticians who prepare these reports use different items to compare costs. For example, many reports use the price of milk to determine how much it costs to live in a particular city. A good indicator, unless you don't drink milk. Take the guides as a rough estimate. No report will be able to tell you exactly how much you'll need to budget. The most effective method is for you to investigate the city personally.

Will a company offer you a salary adjustment to live in one of the more expensive cities? If they do, the adjustment is usually quite modest. Organizations simply cannot pay people large sums of money just because they are located in a more expensive city. Although you will find salaries in New York to be higher than those in Atlanta, they do not offset the cost-of-living differences.

Make sure you check the company's relocation policy fully. At a minimum, you should receive one month's salary to offset the costs associated with moving. Renters or recent college graduates are often offered two weeks' salary. The relocation package should also include the physical movement of your household goods to the new location, and a reasonable length of stay in a hotel while you look for new housing. Two weeks to two months, depending on seniority, is standard. While a relocation allowance is primarily designed to cover such costs as deposits to the phone and gas company, it is used by many companies to help compensate you for the increase in living expenses.

A final point you may wish to negotiate if you are moving to a new location is the sale of your old residence. Paying a larger mortgage on a new home is one thing; having to make two house payments can sink even the most solvent household. Besides, you'll probably need the equity from your old home as a down payment on your new residence. Ask your new employer if they offer a third-party real estate service. Although you may not get quite as much money as you would if you sold your house yourself, you'll get the equity you need for a new residence much quicker by using the service.

Relocating

Many of the same issues emerge if your employer decides to relocate you. Each year American businesses relocate over 250,000 people. While some families are accustomed to picking up and moving every few years, for the majority, relocation is often highly stressful. Fortunately, most companies make a considerable effort to ensure that the move is as painless as possible.

It's certainly not cheap for businesses to relocate their employees. The Employee Relocation Council in Washington, DC, estimates that companies spend over $35,000 to relocate each home-owning worker and $10,000 for renters. Where does this money go? A typical relocation package consists of househunting expenses, financial assistance in obtaining a mortgage, help with closing costs, temporary living expenses, physically moving your household, and other miscellaneous expenses. It's easy to see how the costs of relocating can add up so quickly.

If you're about to be transferred or have accepted a new job in a different area of the country, one of your initial major concerns will be housing. Most companies will allow you and your spouse one or two trips to check out the new city. A smaller number of companies will let you bring your children along. This is something you often need to negotiate.

Ask your employer to recommend the services of a local realtor or relocation consultant. These individuals are invaluable in helping you evaluate schools, home price histories, and the relative desirability of certain neighborhoods. Remember, if you've been transferred once, the odds are high that you will be transferred again. Make sure you purchase a house that should sell quickly when it comes time to move once more.

Generally, in order to buy a new house, you have to sell your existing home first. Companies often offer assistance in this area. Some will purchase your home themselves, others arrange for a third-party relocation firm to buy it. The offer you receive will be based on two or three independent appraisals. On average, you'll have 30 to 90 days in which to accept the offer or decide to sell your house on your own. If you decide to sell your home yourself, you may be able to make more money, but it will take longer. The third-party offer is especially attractive if you're interested in relocating as quickly as possible.

You may be asked to begin work in the new city before your family is relocated. Virtually all employers cover an employee's temporary living expenses, and most also pick up the costs for the entire family. Most companies limit this temporary living assistance to 30 days, although it can sometimes be extended if unforeseen problems occur.

The movement of your furniture and other household items is a standard component of the relocation package. Find out if packing and unpacking boxes is included. This can greatly reduce the hassle associated with moving. Make sure you check out your company's policy on additional insurance coverage for your belongings while they are being moved. A mover's standard policy often does not cover the replacement value of your household goods. It makes good sense to obtain additional coverage even if your employer is not picking up the tab. Since your new house may not be ready precisely when you arrive, also check out your company's policy on temporarily storing your belongings. This is another area that can often be negotiated.

Employees are often surprised at the unanticipated additional costs that crop up as a result of relocation. Items such as auto registrations, appliance hook-ups, carpets, and drapes can add up quickly. To cover these expenses, many companies offer their employees a lump-sum relocation allowance that ranges from two weeks' to one month's pay.

With so many dual-income households, company-sponsored employment assistance to the trailing spouse is a valuable benefit. This may include career counseling, help in preparing résumés, and job lead contacts. Assistance is often provided on an as-needed basis. Don't be shy about inquiring if your spouse's employer can't offer a transfer to your new location.

Although companies are increasingly concerned with their bottom line, most do a good job of trying to help relocated employees adjust to their new surroundings as quickly as possible. Making sure you understand all the provisions in your company's relocation policy can help reduce the stress associated with the move.

CHAPTER 33

MAKING THE TRANSITION FROM A MILITARY CAREER

In the civilian world, duty rosters mean little, and APR refers to annual percentage rate. A former military employee who discusses his or her background using these terms might as well be speaking Chinese. However, if the candidate translates his or her military experience into civilian language and talks about implementing personnel planning and performance appraisal programs, corporate recruiters understand and are impressed.

Making the transition from military to civilian employment poses some unique challenges. Fortunately, the military has implemented a number of programs that can help smooth your transition. Once your separation date has been determined, make sure you schedule a visit to your installation's transition center. These offices are located on most major military bases and are staffed by career advisors who understand the issues veterans face in seeking civilian employment. Center personnel can provide needed assistance in translating your military accomplishments into achievements that are relevant to the civilian world. This is critical if you are to develop and implement a targeted and effective job search campaign.

A helpful tool to assist you in remembering and reviewing your military accomplishments is the computerized statement issued by the Department of Defense which verifies your military experience and training. If, for some reason, you have difficulty obtaining this document, you should conduct your own review of your military career. List all of the positions you held and your primary duties in a chronological format. You may find your fitness evaluations to be helpful in this process. As you develop this list, think about specific accomplishments and achievements. For example, list situations in which you managed materials or resources, supervised others, participated in key decisions, reduced expenditures, improved quality, or increased production. This list will be important in developing your résumé and will help you prepare for face-to-face interviews.

Once you have identified your accomplishments, the next challenge is to determine where your background and skills best fit in the civilian marketplace. This business reference section on your base or in your local library can help you begin to identify potential employers. Other sources you might consider include the Local Veterans Employment Representative, who is located in the state job services or unemployment office. This person's mission is to provide separating and retiring veterans with information on the local job market. Noncommissioned officers might think about contacting the Non Commissioned Officers Association, which sponsors a variety of job fairs throughout the country. This organization also conducts job search workshops and seminars, and operates a computerized résumé listing service. Finally, the Retired Officers Association offers a résumé matching service as a part of its office placement system.

After completing your research, the next step is to market yourself to prospective employers. Career counselors are unanimous in their belief that networking is the most effective method for making contacts at your targeted group of companies. Obviously, some companies will be easier to penetrate than others. Companies that either have a history of hiring former military personnel, such as computer consultant EDS, or military contractors, such as Lockheed, may be most receptive to your networking attempts. If you are stymied in your efforts, don't overlook recruiting firms that specialize in placing former military officers and enlisted people. Many of these firms also conduct career fairs that give you the opportunity to interview with a number of companies in a single day.

You are sure to find the civilian process different than what you experienced in the military. The civilian market places far more emphasis on "fit" then it does on technical qualifications. This can be a source of frustration to former military personnel. For example, interviews in the military are characterized by quick, clipped questions and answers with a heavy emphasis on military jargon. You will have to go against your military instincts when you interview in the civilian market. Don't be afraid to reflect for a moment on the question you are being asked before formulating your answer. Points are given for the content of your answers rather than how fast they are delivered.

Interviews will also expose you to the difference in civilian and military dress code. While in the military you literally wear your position on your sleeve, civilian positions are often shrouded in a blur of gray and blue suits. Thus, make sure you invest in a couple of good-quality suits. Clothing consultants say your initial suit purchases should either be a solid dark gray or a gray pinstripe, but consider the field you will be entering before making a final investment. Men, particularly marines, are also well advised to begin letting their hair grow before embarking on face-to-face interviews. One of the important tenets of interviewing is to blend in with the work environment.

There are a number of unique challenges facing exiting military personnel, but with planning and forethought, your background can be positioned successfully and the unique advantages of your military experience positively communicated.

CHAPTER 34

ESTABLISHING A BUSINESS PARTNERSHIP

As reorganizations and downsizings continue to wreck havoc on the ranks of middle managers, many individuals are investigating entrepreneurial or small business ventures. It's easy to understand why this career option has become increasingly popular. Losing your job can make you highly cynical about ever working for a large corporation again. This is especially true for people who have spent the majority of their careers with a single employer. Thus, the prospect of working for themselves becomes highly appealing.

If you've thought about starting your own business, you've probably also thought, "Should I go it alone or bring in a partner?" As with any business decision, there are both good and bad reasons for setting up a partnership. If you enter into the relationship for the right reasons you can significantly increase your likelihood of business success. Conversely, partnerships that are formed in haste or for the wrong reasons can torpedo even the most promising ventures.

The first question you've got to ask yourself is, "Why do I need a partner?" Partnerships are typically formed for either financial, companionship, or expertise reasons. Of these, the last usually leads to the healthiest and most successful relationship. The ideal partnership is one where your skills are complementary, but not identical, to those of your partner. For example, you may have skills in finance and accounting, while your partner is good at marketing and sales. Make sure you take the time to fully discuss who will be responsible for what. By establishing separate turf areas, you can avoid much of the friction that plagues many business partnerships.

While expertise may be the best reason for establishing a partnership, there is no denying that any business idea will die on the vine without money. Unfortunately, many budding entrepreneurs enter financial partnership arrangements that prove disastrous.

As any small business advisor will tell you, before you start your business, you'll need to develop a business plan. Although this roadmap will change somewhat over time, a business plan will help you determine how much money you're going to need to get the business off the ground. If your personal savings are inadequate, meet with a loan officer at the bank with which you do business. Depending on the type of business you're proposing, you may be surprised at the officer's level of receptivity. Your banker can also advise you on other sources of financing, such as Small Business Administration (SBA) loans. Unfortunately, visiting the local bank is a step many individuals forget. If you can strike a deal here, it will be far preferable to entering into a relationship with a financial partner.

A financial partner will want a significant stake in your business as an incentive to invest. In some cases, you may have to give up majority ownership. He or she will also look for a return of at least 20 percent on his or her investment, which may force you to expand your business faster than you want. Many small business owners forget that their financial partner also has a business philosophy. Make sure you find out what that philosophy is up front. If you select a partner carefully, the relationship can be mutually beneficial. The key is getting to know your financier as a businessperson rather than just a checkbook.

By far the worst reason to enter into a business partnership is for companionship. Yet countless partnerships start out for precisely this reason, and it's easy to see why. As most self-employed individuals will tell you, loneliness is the most significant downside of being out on your own. The lure of bonding with another individual through establishing a business partnership is powerful. Unfortunately, it seldom works out. Just because I like you doesn't mean we will be good business partners. In fact, the history of business is filled with highly successful partnerships in which the principals didn't much care for each other. Loneliness is a real issue but is usually better alleviated by joining associations and civic groups than by establishing a business partnership.

A frank exchange of views between you and your prospective partner is crucial for your relationship to work. Spell out who will be responsible for what, how fast you want the business to grow, which markets you are going to target, and how large a business you want to create. Finally, don't forget to discuss the worst case scenario—what you're going to do if the venture doesn't work out. In the enthusiasm to start a new relationship, people often forget to establish how they will dissolve the partnership, should it become necessary. Business partnerships are like a marriage. If they work out, there is nothing better; if they don't, there's nothing worse.

CHAPTER 35

WORKING PART-TIME

Not everyone wants to work full-time. A common question job seekers ask is, "Should I take a part-time job if I'm having difficulty finding full-time employment?" There are several issues to consider before making this decision. Accepting a part-time position can either needlessly drag out your search for full-time employment or be the stepping-stone to the perfect job.

Whether a part-time job is right for you depends on your reasons for considering this option. Being out of work places a great deal of stress on you and your family. If a job search drags on for months, you begin to wonder if you'll ever again find a full-time job. The tension level between you and your spouse begins to rise. You can hardly be blamed for thinking that any job would be better than continued unemployment. However, taking a part-time job for these reasons is usually a mistake. Jobs individuals often consider at this point include working for a retail store or selling real estate. The latter is particularly appealing since people perceive this business as an easy way to make a few bucks. Nothing could be farther from the truth.

Real estate normally pays its salespeople on a 100 percent commission basis. It will take many months for you to become established and see any money coming in. Retail jobs typically pay minimum wage, and you can expect to work long hours, including weekends.

The chief disadvantage of taking part-time jobs such as these is that they take time away from your full-time job search. As much as you try to convince yourself that you will continue to budget time for the search you are likely to find that these good intentions go unfulfilled. Since most people dislike the process of looking for work, they use any excuse to avoid doing the things they know they should be doing. A part-time job will provide you with a veritable feast of reasons not to look for full-time work. The end result is that your part-time job is unfulfilling, your full-time job search stagnates, and you wind up more frustrated than ever.

On the other hand, it's impossible to deny the financial realities of being out of work. The concern for family finances is one of the primary reasons people consider part-time work in the first place. Since few families have any sort of formal budget, it is important that you establish one as soon as possible. You may discover that your finances are not as bleak as you feared. This can reduce the pressure you may be feeling to rush out and get a part-time job just to keep the wolves from the door.

If you decide you need a part-time job, try to find one in your field. These jobs can often open up doors to full-time employment and deserve close scrutiny.

In absolute terms, the number of part-time opportunities continues to grow due to the restructurings still taking place within many industries. Companies that laid off hundreds of employees are very nervous about having to repeat the process. However, since work still needs to get done, the solution is to expand the temporary workforce. Today, some part-time workers log so many hours with a particular company that they are referred to as "full-time temporaries."

Finding Part-Time Jobs

Finding part-time jobs can be done in any of three ways. Check with the local office of your trade or professional association. If you're not sure which association you should belong to, ask the research librarian at your local public library for the *Directory of Associations*. This volume will provide you with information on associations by industry and function. Many of the larger ones have in-house job referral programs and can tell you how to learn about part-time jobs in your field.

A number of employment agencies also specialize in part-time jobs. While many of these agencies specialize in temporary assignments for clerical, accounting, and data processing workers, an increasing number are now placing professionals in a variety of fields.

Finally, you should apply directly to companies in which you have an interests. Many larger corporations have in-house temporary services and are interested in learning about individuals with a variety of skills.

You should be aware that accepting any part-time assignment does present some risks. You may not be covered under the company's benefit plan, and part-time employees are the first to be let go if business turns soft. However, since there is the possibility that the part-time job will turn into a full-time position, this option may be worth considering for some job seekers.

The Freelancing Option

In an ongoing effort to balance lifestyle and career commitments, more and more people are investigating the option of becoming freelance employees.

Freelancing provides individuals with the opportunity to control their own destiny but makes demands for which many people are not prepared.

Freelancers generally offer services in an area of expertise which they developed as a part of their regular job or as the result of an outside hobby. For example, a former sales manager may provide freelance expertise by training salespeople for several companies, while an individual whose hobby is gourmet cooking may begin a freelance operation offering cooking classes and catering services.

One of the challenges facing freelancers is obtaining clients. In some cases, freelancers subcontract with larger organizations offering similar services. Many large consulting firms, for example, need freelance consultants to assist with projects for large clients. Your public library should have a copy of the *Directory of Management Consulting Firms*, which lists these organizations by location and area of expertise. Another option is to subcontract your services with a major corporation. For example, former corporate staffing managers can now be found in a number of companies working as freelance recruiters.

There are certainly a number of advantages to becoming a freelancer. Freelancers work only on those assignments in which they have an interest and enjoy more independence than company employees. Independence is probably one of the major reasons people become freelancers in the first place. Once you have experienced this degree of freedom, it may be difficult to ever go back to the corporate world. If independence is very important to you, freelancing may be a highly rewarding career choice.

Most freelancers work out of their homes. This can be both a blessing and a curse. A home-based business allows you to operate a minimum amount of additional overhead and the commute to "work" can hardly be beat. Conversely, household chores can distract you from the business task that must be performed if your freelance effort is to be successful. You need to be highly disciplined in order not to fall into unproductive habits such as watching television rather than making the phone calls necessary to drum up new business. A number of freelancers comment on how important it is to dress as if they are going to work. Although it isn't necessary to wear a suit, if you lounge around all day in your pajamas or sweats, you are likely to accomplish little more than lounging around all day. (For more information see Chapter 36.)

From a financial perspective, freelancing also has its upside and downside. If you are effective at marketing your services, you may find yourself earning more than you did previously. However, you need to be aware that the income stream will be uneven. You may make a lot of money one month and then go several months without billing a client. This can make paying self-employment taxes and health insurance premiums difficult. A willingness to get paid in periodic clumps with no guarantee of future earnings is one of the adjustments freelancers must make, and it demands savvy financial planning.

A financial benefit to freelancing is that many of your expenses may be tax deductible. For example, if you have one room of your house devoted *solely* to your freelance activities, it can often be written off your taxes. Make sure you seek the advice of a trained accountant to maximize your tax deductions.

Keep in mind that all of your expenses, overhead, and insurance will have to be paid out of the money you earn. This can often come as a shock. Remember, there are no company benefit programs for freelancers. Check with an independent insurance agent on the best health coverage for yourself and your family. Although you may find the premiums high, they are cheap compared to the costs of incurring a serious illness without insurance.

Perhaps the most frustrating aspect of freelancing is the inherent loneliness and uncertainty that is part of the lifestyle. Many individuals never realized how important it was to be able to "drop in and see what Jerry was up to" until they no longer had anyone to drop in on. Not having someone with whom to discuss ideas or commiserate can prove discouraging and rob freelancers of their motivation. You can satisfy this need for human interaction by joining both social and professional organizations. In addition to being a source of camaraderie, memberships can often pay significant networking dividends.

Even the most successful freelancers know they cannot predict their level of activity beyond a few months. Although you may be overwhelmed with work today, three months down the road you may be without an assignment. As one freelancer says, "Business is great, but I'm not worried." Thus, it is critical that you keep you fixed expenses as low as possible. Knowing that you have three to six months of living expenses in the bank can give you the confidence to keep going when you experience a temporary lack of work.

While freelancing can provide enormous career satisfaction and independence, it is a little like the circus performer who works without a net. It is usually an option best suited to those individuals who are stout of heart and have a skill that can be readily marketed and is in demand.

Flex-time and Job Sharing

A third option you might consider is to enter into a flex-time arrangement with your boss. Again, there are some unique issues you need to be aware of.

For many years, we've been reading stories about job sharing and flexible schedules. On the surface, the concept sounds great. Flexible schedules should enable people who otherwise might opt to drop out of the workforce to continue in their jobs. However, questions still remain. Has the concept really been embraced by the business community? What impact does a part-time job have on your long-term career prospects? From an employer's viewpoint, what are the benefits and liabilities of such an arrangement?

The consensus among employment observers is that there's more hype than substance to these new employer-employee relationships. Although job sharing and other part-time work arrangements are a good concept, they haven't been used extensively yet. Part of the employers' reluctance may be due to the newness of the concept. It's often difficult to get managers to view your commitment to work positively when it's less than 100 percent. Part-time work relationships appear to be contradictory in these times of reorganizations and layoffs when most companies are asking workers to do more with less.

Individuals most interested in part-time work are often new parents who are attempting to achieve more balance in their lives. Despite the much-ballyhooed concept of "Mr. Mom," women still tend to take the primary child-rearing role. However, these women are often highly educated and have held professional positions with considerable responsibility. While they don't want to completely retire from the workforce, they also aren't willing to make the 100 percent commitment to their careers that they made right out of school. Under the right circumstances, a part-time work position can be mutually beneficial for both these individuals and their employers.

A case in point is the example of Ellie Thompson. After graduating from Emory with an MBA, Ellie embarked on a career in marketing with Kraft Foods in Chicago. After returning to Atlanta and giving birth to her daughter, Ellie decided that although she still wanted to work, she also wanted the flexibility to spend time with her child. After investigating a number of alternatives, Ellie now job-shares a position at Emory with another woman. While she earns less than she did before, she now has the balance she desired in her life.

The success of a part-time arrangement largely depends on how your supervisor feels about the concept. Opinions on the merits of part-time work vary considerably. One of the primary concerns you're likely to face is a fear that you won't be accessible to co-workers or customers. Fortunately, computers and other office technology can alleviate many of these problems. In Ellie Thompson's case, a telephone beeper, computer, and e-mail enable her to provide the necessary level of service to her co-workers and clients. Greg Gesse, Ellie's boss, makes the point that the supervisor needs to adopt a new attitude toward managing people: "Overall, I'm very pleased with the relationship. It enabled us to staff the position with a caliber of professional that we might not otherwise be able to attract."

A willingness to give and take is important for any part-time relationship to work. You may find you can't be wedded to only working specific hours on specific days. On some days, you may need to put in a little more time; on others, you can cut back. However, it's important that you monitor your time and avoid the trap of being so willing to take on new assignments that you eventually work full-time hours. This is another reason the relationship between you and your boss is so important.

Some supervisors may be concerned that part-time work will become so popular, other workers will ask for similar treatment. From a practical standpoint, most companies can only handle a limited number of part-time workers and still maintain productivity. While co-workers may be envious of the part-timer's flexibility, they need to remember that the part-time person is making considerably less money, and may no longer be entitled to company benefits.

If you're considering part-time work, you might investigate the non-profit sector of the employment market. These organizations appear to be the most open-minded about nontraditional working arrangements. However, that doesn't mean your current employer won't be interested in considering you for a part-time job. Remember, though, that you'll probably have to initiate the conversation.

CHAPTER 36

WORKING FROM HOME

An increasing number of businesspeople are working out of their homes. A survey conducted by *The New York Times* in 1992 estimated that over 39 million people worked out of their homes either full- or part-time. Economists anticipate that this number will only increase in the future.

Working out of your home has both benefits and drawbacks. For one thing, it's hard to beat the commute. With the availability of fax machines, computers, modems, and multi-line telephones, you can operate a fairly sophisticated office from the comfort of an extra bedroom. You can wear what you want and you will normally be able to experience a high level of flexibility in your daily schedule. If you have young children, a part-time home-based business allows you to spend more time with them.

So, what's the downside? Many home-based workers cite loneliness as the number one problem. You may never realize how important dropping in on a co-worker was until you no longer have that option. While independence and flexibility are the plus side of the equation, it takes a certain type of strong-willed, disciplined individual to successfully function in the home environment. Another issue is that while procrastination is a challenge for all of us, it is especially difficult for people working out of their homes.

There is also the disadvantage that others may not view a home-based business as a "real" business. The decision to start working out of your home sometimes can put a strain on a marriage, since your spouse may erroneously conclude that you'll have extra time available to accomplish a plethora of domestic chores.

Still, for those who are able to manage the unique challenges a home-based business offers, the rewards are considerable. To increase your odds of success you need to be aware of some fundamental rules of etiquette that can help you over the rough spots.

A Place of Your Own

Make sure you have a room devoted to your business. Setting up shop in the space next to the washer and dryer is a recipe for disaster. The space should be restricted to work activities, and you need to be diligent about keeping other (family) demands from intruding on this space. Allowing your home office to become a communal family activity area makes your ability to function as a "real" businessperson all the more difficult. If possible, try to have your home office located in an area of the house that's off the beaten track. The more you can physically distance your office from the flow of daily family traffic, the better. Converting space in the garage, basement, or attic worked well for some people.

Have at least one separate phone line run into your office. Access to a telephone is critical for success. You don't want to compete for the phone with other family members. Since you'll probably want to have a modem or fax machine as a part of your business, you may find that two separate business lines are necessary. You'll want to make sure you invest wisely in your telephone system, since it will be the primary link between you and the outside business world.

Getting Dressed

No, you don't have to wear a suit and tie or a dress to your home office (unless you really want to), but you don't want to spend the day in your pajamas, either. Although your daily dress is likely to be casual (most home-based workers recommend that you don't deny yourself this pleasure), make sure you forgo the casual look when calling on clients and customers. Wearing jeans all day can sometimes make you forget that the rest of the business world doesn't have the same flexibility in dress code you do. Make sure you keep your hair length consistent with a conservative business image and don dressy clothes when it's appropriate. Another advantage of working from your home is that you probably won't be wearing traditional business attire as often, and, consequently, you suits are likely to last a good deal longer.

Getting Out

There's no denying that loneliness is a real problem for the home-based worker, so, make sure you take proactive steps to get out of the office each day. Simple trips to the bank or post office can help you avoid feeling like a hermit. Make sure you're away from the office at least once a day, if not more.

Professional and trade associations are a blessing for the home-based businessperson. Yes, a lot of the speakers are boring, and you'll tend to run into the same people time and time again, but association meetings offer both a good reason to get out of the house and the possibility of developing meaningful networking contacts. Social skills, like any other set of skills, can get rusty without use. If nothing else, attending association meetings allows you to keep those skills in proper order.

Establishing Office Hours

Another issue facing the home-based worker is not allowing adequate time off for rest, recreation, and family activities. This is why it is so important to set regular office hours. One of the advantages of working at home is that you may be able to adapt the requirements of your work day to meet your individual needs. A number of home-based workers report that their schedules are quite different than when they worked in an office environment. For example, Paul Scott, a home-based systems engineer in Dallas, Texas, states, "I generally get up around 7:00 A.M. and read the morning papers for an hour. I then spend the next hour and a half exercising, getting dressed, and cooking breakfast. I'm at my desk by 9:30. Since I'm most productive in the evenings, my business day generally doesn't end before 7:30."

Whatever schedule you choose, make sure you stick with it. Many home-based workers report a tendency to work too many, rather than too few, hours. Since there are no hours in which you have to be at work, it's not uncommon to feel that you should be at work all the time.